10 0065917 5

KU-533-654

WITHDRAWN

Claude Michelet

La Grande Muraille

James Dryhurst

Senior Lecturer in French
University of Leeds

UNIVERSITY OF GLASGOW
FRENCH AND GERMAN PUBLICATIONS
1996

NOTTINGHAM
UNIVERSITY LIBRARY

University of Glasgow French and German Publications

Series Editors: Mark G. Ward (German)
Geoff Woollen (French)

Consultant Editors: Colin Smethurst
Kenneth Varty

Modern Languages Building, University of Glasgow,
Glasgow G12 8QL, Scotland.

———•———

À la mémoire de David Michelet,
volontaire de la FORPRONU en Bosnie.

———•———

First published 1996.

© Copyright UNIVERSITY of GLASGOW FRENCH & GERMAN PUBLICATIONS.

All rights reserved. No part of this publication may be reproduced,
stored in a retrieval system, or transmitted, in any form or by any
means, electronical, mechanical, recording or otherwise, without the
prior permission of the publisher.

Printed by Jasprint Ltd., Washington, Tyne & Wear.

ISBN 0 85261 527 2

Contents

1000659175 T

Preface

Claude Michelet is one of the most popular writers in France. The sales of his books run into millions, and his best-known novels, *Des grives aux loups* and *Les Palombes ne passeront plus,* have been turned into highly successful films for television and translated into many languages. The extent of his talent was already visible in *La Grande Muraille,* which he considers to be his first real novel. It was originally published in 1969 in a small edition by Julliard, but the author later moved to the publishing house of Robert Laffont, that has since published all his novels (though not all of his other books).

As well as being well worth reading and studying in its own right, *La Grande Muraille* provides an excellent introduction to Claude Michelet's other works. The latter are briefly presented here in the hope of encouraging readers to try them for themselves. Apart from newspaper and other reviews of his works, and two articles in *Francophonie,* the only work on Michelet of which I am aware is *Claude Michelet sur la terre des hommes,* by his friend Pierre Panen. I am greatly indebted both to him and to his book. Although written as a presentation to a wider reading audience than that of an academic study, it contains pertinent comment on his works, as well as biographical and other information, and is now out in paperback.

I am extremely grateful to Claude and Bernadette Michelet for the warm and generous welcome which they gave to my wife and myself at Marcillac in August, 1994, and for showing us the wall which served as the inspiration for the novel. Information given during our interview is referred to in the text by the abbreviated *Int.* Books and articles quoted are listed by title and number in the bibliography and referred to by number (in italics) in the text—e.g. (*3,* p. 46). Page numbers by themselves in **bold** typeface refer to the current Presses Pocket edition (no. 1999) of *La Grande Muraille.*

I should like to acknowledge here the study leave and travel grant given to me for the purposes of this work by the University of Leeds French Department. I wish also to thank all my colleagues in the Department for their help and encouragement, notably Margaret Atack, Philip Thody, David Coward, Howard Evans, David Platten, Jim House, Andrew Rothwell and Christopher Todd. The assistance of Jean Murgatroyd, Arts Computing Officer, has been invaluable. The debt I owe to my wife, Patricia, for her expert advice as a sixth-form teacher and for her constant love and support during the whole process of producing this little book, is an enormous one.

Chapter One

The making of a writer

La Grande Muraille was first published in 1969. It is the story of an agricultural worker in a remote part of rural France who spends his life building an apparently useless wall over a period of forty years or more, starting just before the First World War and ending in the mid-1950s. The story is an unusual one and the career of its author, Claude Michelet, has been equally unusual. Unlike the stereotypical French author, an academic or a civil servant following purely intellectual pursuits in Paris, he worked full time, until his health no longer allowed it, as a farmer living in the part of France in which the book is set. This has led some critics to look down on or ignore him. I hope that this little study will help to prove them wrong.

Claude Michelet does not correspond to the usual stereotype as a farmer any more than he does as a writer. His family background was urban, but as a child he had learned to love the countryside and this triggered a passionate desire to be a farmer. He received an excellent agricultural training as well as a good general education and this enabled him both to analyse and to face on a practical level the immensely complex problems that modern agriculture poses, not only for the farmer but for the whole of our economic and ecological system. At the time when *La Grande Muraille* appeared, his surname was nationally known, for his father had until recently been a government minister—France was just emerging from the near revolution produced by the student riots of May 1968—and was soon to be a minister again. Most people, therefore, would have thought that his youngest son would be working in a carpeted office rather than in a cowshed or a muddy field, but Claude was in the cowshed not by chance but from choice, and the rural environment in which he lived was a natural one in which to situate his first novel.

Living where he did in the Corrèze gave him not only an excellent knowledge of the village life which figures so largely in *La Grande Muraille* but also, more importantly, a deep understanding of it. Besides this, he had an excellent knowledge of, and a feel for, the historical events which serve as the background to the novel— notably the two world wars. He had gained this knowledge not only

from his education and from his reading but also from his own and
other people's direct experience.

One important source for the earlier part of the book was his own
family. When the First World War broke out in 1914, his father,
Edmond Michelet, would have loved to volunteer for service, but
was not old enough to join the army until the war was nearly over.
He eventually did join it, as a volunteer, so he was kept on for
service in the post-war period. Although the slaughter of the
trenches was over, many of those he served with had lived through
what Firmin and his fictional namesake Edmond undergo in *La
Grande Muraille* and were able to tell him of their experiences, as
was many another ex-soldier that both he and Claude later met.

The collective experience of the Michelet family was also a clear
source of help as regards another important aspect of *La Grande
Muraille*, namely the political and religious one. We are told that in
1914 the village of Les Landes was fiercely republican (7). We may,
at the end of the twentieth century, find it hard to think of France as
having any other form of government than a republic, but in 1914
some Frenchmen, mostly Catholics, still hankered after a monarchy.
Indeed France at the time had spent most of the previous hundred
years under one kind of monarch or another; it was only in 1870 that
the Third Republic had been declared. As well as implying
opposition to aristocrats such as the Austrian archduke murdered in
Sarajevo (7), the term 'republican' in early twentieth-century France
also held a strong implication of anticlericalism; such is the case with
many of the village's inhabitants, and notably with Firmin.

The struggle between clericals and anticlericals in France
antedates the 1789 Revolution and has at many times since then been
extremely virulent. The Catholic Church's position as the established
church had been confirmed in 1802 by Napoleon in a Concordat with
the Pope and was further strengthened under the restored Bourbon
monarchy in the early nineteenth century. Many people, however,
resented the Church's power and influence, particularly in the matter
of education, and the long dispute dragged on through the nineteenth
century, culminating in a series of anticlerical laws, passed by the
politicians of the Third Republic at the end of that century and the
beginning of the twentieth, which formally separated Church and
State. Like other Catholics at the time, Edmond Michelet's parents
felt deeply hurt by these laws. They considered them to be unjust,
since they involved, amongst other provisions, the expulsion from
France of many priests and nuns and their resentment was all the

greater in view of the financial scandals with which some of the politicians who passed those laws were associated.

For their part, the anticlericals felt that at last the Church's power and influence were being cut down to size and that a threat to their personal freedom had been removed. In 1894 the Dreyfus Affair, in which a Jewish officer in the French army had been falsely accused and convicted of spying for the Germans, had further embittered the question. The affair went on for a dozen years and its divisive effects persisted long afterwards. Many Catholics, particularly on the political right wing, took sides against Dreyfus. Others supported him and were vindicated when he was finally proved innocent in 1906, but the damage had been done and the term 'clerical' tended to be seen as synonymous with 'anti-Dreyfus'. At local level the ideological gap between clericals and anticlericals could be wide and was deeply felt. It tended, over many years, to take the form of a battle between the *curé* and the *instituteur*. The divide is clearly visible in the village community in *La Grande Muraille*. There, however, it does not embitter personal relationships, as it often did elsewhere, both before and after 1914. This is largely due to the wise and tolerant personality of the old *curé* and that of his successor Edmond. In that, their parish is a fairly unusual one. The attitude of tolerance which reigns there corresponds to Claude Michelet's own views and reflects both the atmosphere in which he was brought up and the influence exerted on him by his father. That influence was, and is, a very powerful one, and understandably so. There are many manifestations of it in *La Grande Muraille*.

Tolerance on both sides of the divide had to be learned. In that learning process, the First World War had an important part to play, despite, or perhaps rather because of, all its horrors. The comradeship of the trenches often brought reconciliation and friendship, without loss of principle, between people of differing views. This often outlasted the war, as it does in the case of Firmin and his cousin. Time also brought about changes in people. Thus Edmond Michelet had been a royalist, both before and after the 1914-1918 War, and indeed for a time was involved with the extremist Charles Maurras, but left his movement because of its advocacy of violence and moved towards more liberal views. Others on both left and right did the same, but much later on in most cases. Edmond was active in several purely Catholic bodies and then became deeply committed, during the nineteen-thirties, to an organisation called *Les Équipes sociales*. This was a self-help movement with a network of local branches which brought together people of all creeds and persuasions, many of whom had served in the war. Its aim was mutual help, especially in the fields of education and job-training, and it played its part in fighting the effects of the terrible economic depression which affected France, and the rest of the world, during the thirties.

In addition to these activities, Edmond, having married Marie Vialle, the daughter of a well-known doctor in Brive, had by now a large family to bring up—Claude was the youngest of seven. As a very committed Catholic, he was also engaged, in the years leading up to the Second World War, in trying to move local and national church opinion away from its old backward-looking attitudes, notably in the matter of social justice. The Church at that time was obsessed with the dangers of Communism, as exemplified by Soviet Russia, but Edmond and his associates, at both local and national level, also tried to draw attention to the dangers to human rights posed by the rise of Nazism and Fascism; the régimes of Hitler and Mussolini were by now well established. Indeed, as early as March 1933, an article, with photographs, had appeared in the popular magazine *Lectures pour tous* on the subject of the newly opened concentration camp at Dachau, with which Edmond was later to become only too familiar. Unfortunately these warnings were ignored until it was too late, and not just by people within the Church. When war came, some priests were willing to join the Resistance, as Edmond does in *La Grande Muraille,* but they were relatively few in number; so were recruits from the rest of the population. The fictional Edmond, like the author's father, is an exceptional person.

The Second World War broke out in September 1939. Edmond was then living in Brive with his family and working as a commercial traveller. The collapse of the French forces under Hitler's sudden attack in May 1940 horrified him and Pétain's surrender filled him with disgust. He felt he had at least to make some kind of gesture in reply, so he assembled some friends, mostly from the *Équipes Sociales*, and together they stencilled copies of a leaflet and pushed them through the letter boxes of Brive. The leaflet consisted of extracts from *L'Argent,* by Charles Péguy, a poet with a strong mystical and patriotic streak who was killed in 1914, in the first weeks of war, and who was a lasting influence on both Edmond and on Claude Michelet. The source may have been poetic, but its central message was brave and crystal clear:

En temps de guerre, celui qui ne se rend pas est mon homme, quel qu'il soit, d'où qu'il vienne et quel que soit son parti (28, p. 1187).

This symbolic gesture, carried out on 17 June 1940, the day before the then little-known General de Gaulle's famous call to France to continue the fight was broadcast by the B.B.C., marked the start of a distinguished career in the Resistance. Most French people at the time felt completely lost and accepted Marshal Pétain's armistice with the Germans as being the only way out. However, when Edmond heard of de Gaulle and his call to resist, he immediately associated himself both with him and with his ideal of putting aside partisan interests, whether of left or right, so as to unite for the national good. Edmond in fact was a natural Gaullist; he had held similar views, inspired by Péguy, for many years (5, pp. 32-3) and was to support the General for the rest of his life. Claude Michelet shares his father's Gaullist ideals, but has always consistently refused to join the party political rat race as a candidate.

Another of Edmond's early gestures of resistance was to oblige the mayors of local villages to replace the bust of Marianne, the symbol of the Republic, on its plinth in the *mairie* from which they had illegally removed it. There is a possible echo of this in Firmin's criticism of the portrait of Pétain which suddenly appears in the village *bistrot* after the 1940 armistice (**126**) and in the flowers in patriotic colours which appear there and in the *mairie* with equal suddenness after the Liberation (**143-4**). Edmond Michelet's gestures were soon followed by more solid action. By the end of 1940, he had set up a fully-fledged Resistance group, 'Liberté', made up of people of all political and religious persuasions, and when the national Resistance movement 'Combat' came into being in 1941, he was put in command of his local region, the Fifth, covering several *départements*. Edmond was thus involved in setting up the future secret army which eventually allowed Brive to be the first French town to liberate itself from the Germans, who surrendered to the local French forces there on 15 August 1944.

Edmond managed to remain active in the Resistance as an organiser and as an explosives expert until early in 1943. He was able to do so because, like his namesake in the book, he took every possible precaution. He also used his image as a harmless idealist to fend off suspicion. He made no secret of his Gaullist views, but no one thought that the pious, well-respected father of a large family could be an active *résistant*. In the novel, however, Firmin expresses his views much too loudly for his cousin to be able to risk involving him in his own Resistance activities (**128-9**) and the loud-mouthed young *maquisards* pay with their lives for being careless (**133**). Betrayal was a constant danger in the Resistance, however careful the precautions were. When the German foraging party arrives in the village, Edmond fears he may have been denounced by 'le petit Hervé' (**134**) and asks Firmin, unnecessarily as it turns out, to warn the others in his unit about a possible traitor. In real life, Edmond Michelet was not so lucky; in his case betrayal was followed by arrest. Fortunately the Germans did not realise exactly who and what Edmond was, and he kept silent under torture, so his comrades were saved and he, instead of being executed, was sent to Dachau concentration camp in south Germany. This was not an extermination camp as such, but conditions were appalling and inhuman and very many prisoners died there of ill treatment, overwork, hunger or disease. Edmond was to spend two years in Dachau, surviving many privations and beatings as well as the dreaded typhus fever.

His father's first-hand experiences and his own boyhood memories of the period have enabled Claude Michelet to write with considerable authority about the Resistance, both in *La Grande Muraille* and in other works. He had been born in 1938 in Brive, in the Corrèze. With his six older brothers and sisters, he spent his early childhood between the family house there and a farmhouse at Marcillac, a *lieu-dit* (i.e. a place with a name, the lowest rung on a hierarchical ladder which rises via the *hameau*, the *village* and the *bourg* to culminate in the *ville*). The small group of houses called Marcillac which lies six kilometres to the south of Brive is not to be confused with the better-known and larger villages of Marcillac-la-Croisille and Marcillac-la-Croze, which are also in the Corrèze. The house and its adjoining land, which was let to a local farmer at the time, was all that remained of a larger farm which had belonged to Claude's mother. It was there that he developed his great love of the country, both during early childhood and, later on, during school holidays from Paris. The family stayed in the Corrèze, either at Marcillac or in Brive, throughout the Occupation. It was in Brive that the five-year-old Claude was playing with two of his brothers in their parents' bed early one morning when the Gestapo came to arrest his father. Even to this day he can still hear the sound of the car driving away (*3*, p. 46). The family house where the arrest took place is now a Musée de la Résistance et de la Déportation (see Bibliography for further details).

After Edmond's arrest, the family, living sometimes in Brive and sometimes in Marcillac, tried its best to live as it had done before. They sheltered refugees and carried out whatever other acts of resistance they could; the elder children even embroidered Union Jacks and *croix de Lorraine* on their pullovers and used their pocket money to buy a toy printing set with which they made anti-Nazi leaflets to put through letter boxes on the way to and from school (*3*, pp. 49-50). While in Marcillac, they had a visit from a German foraging party, in much the same way as Firmin's village does (**133-7**). They also had a brush with the S.S., whom Edmond euphemistically refers to as being very different from the milder Wehrmacht (**138**). The children and their mother were trying to cross the road near Marcillac as a long line of German tanks was going past; one of them pointed its gun at them as they ran across. The tanks were from the 'Das Reich' S.S. Panzer division heading north towards the Normandy battlefront. What Edmond says in the novel is prophetic, for on their way, troops from this division committed appalling atrocities against the civilian population, notably at Tulle and in the village of Oradour-sur-Glane, where almost the whole population of over six hundred was massacred.

Schooling was difficult during the war, and Claude received his first lessons from his elder sisters. They in turn were learning via correspondence courses. Their young pupil learned to read at an early age, mainly from old numbers of *L'Illustration* dating from the 1914-1918 war (*Int*). They produced in him a fascination with the history of that period and gave him a detailed knowledge of all the campaigns and battles, later to be augmented, as we have seen, by aural sources and by study. Many acounts of the fighting appear in the novels, but they do not glorify war, as the grisly details of hand-to-hand warfare in the trenches given in *La Grande Muraille* testify (**67**). Almost as soon as Firmin is called up (**54**), he is thrown into action in the battle of the Marne (September 1914). It was thanks to French resistance there that the initial German assault was held and repulsed after getting within thirty-five kilometres of Paris. The Marne also entered into legend as well as history, because reinforcements for the hard-pressed infantry were brought up from the nearby capital by a fleet of over a thousand taxis lent for the occasion by their owners. Later on, Firmin and Edmond are posted to the front near Verdun (**69**), a town in Eastern France whose name is also legendary, but for a different reason. In 1916, the whole area was the scene of a horrendous battle which lasted for many months and in which the French lost over half of their troops, including 221,000 dead; German losses were also enormous. In the novel, both cousins survive this battle, although Edmond is seriously wounded. Clearly they were amongst the lucky ones.

Claude's father finally returned from Dachau after it was liberated by the Americans in May, 1945, but the boy, now seven, did not recognise the emaciated figure, clothed in rags, that he saw (*3*, p. 110). His childhood had in many ways been hard, and at times traumatic. Pierre Panen quotes his reply to a child who asked him about his childhood pranks: 'Tu sais, je n'ai jamais eu de véritable enfance. Je suis né vieux' (*25*, p. 31). But he never lacked affection. Edmond's return was not just a family affair, for he was now a national hero. In November 1945 he was invited to join the provisional government that was set up under De Gaulle and he was to remain in the world of politics for the rest of his life. He was, as we have seen, a natural and ardent Gaullist, but, unlike many other politicians, he entered politics because of a genuine desire to serve his country, not in order to further his own interests.

For the Michelet children, their father's elevation to office in 1945 meant moving to Paris and a completely new lifestyle. As Ministre des armées, Edmond had an official residence in the Ministère de la Marine, looking out over the Place de la Concorde. The arrival of the children there brought new experiences both for them and for the Ministry's naval personnel. They are detailed in *Une fois sept* (*3*, pp. 116-29). Life for Claude was fun, but soon he had to go to school, and that was a much less happy experience. The tone was set on the first day when a teacher slapped his face for looking at a picture on the wall during the lesson. Claude soon developed a strategy for survival in school which consisted of doing just the necessary minimum. He went to several other schools over the years, but it made little real difference, for his heart was not in his studies, though he clearly did not lack ability.

What lay at the root of the problem was that he was missing the countryside of his beloved Corrèze and was gradually becoming horrified at the idea of having to live and work for the rest of his life in Paris (*7*, pp. 28-9). He came to realise that he really wanted to learn to be a farmer, and he finally announced this to his father, whose reaction is recorded on the first page of *J'ai choisi la Terre:*

> Si, un jour, un de mes fils, vers l'âge de douze ans, m'explique avec sérieux que son plus grand désir est de choisir le métier de mineur de fond, sans doute serais-je aussi étonné que le fut mon père.

Despite the initial shock, his father took him seriously, but waited some months in order to test his son's vocation. He then made a considerable act of faith by agreeing to his request.

The college that Edmond chose for Claude, at Lancôme-en-Brenne, to the west of Châteauroux (Indre), was excellent. It combined a training in practical farming with appropriate theoretical studies and a very sound general education. Although the future novelist had been a reluctant pupil at school, he had not been a backward one; his marks for French were very good, even if those for spelling were not. Once at Lancôme, the picture changed completely. He enjoyed not only studying agricultural theory and practice, but also the more conventional subjects, which were taken to a level equivalent to that of the *baccalauréat*. Motivation was now no longer a problem. When his course at Lancôme came to an end, Claude was seventeen. In time he was to take over the farm at Marcillac, so he spent a year working there under a local 'caretaker' farmer. He became so horrified by the man's backwardness, however—he disobeyed most of the lessons that Claude had learned at college—that he returned to Lancôme for another year, gaining experience as a paid *stagiaire* (7, p. 53). Then, to widen his experience still further, he went to work on a very large farm near Paris, but there the mean-mindedness of the employers was matched only by the surliness which it produced in the workers; it was to be the model for a similar farm in *Des grives aux loups*. Filled with disgust, Claude packed his bags and went back to the Corrèze (7, p. 57).

When he was called up for his national service in mid-1958, his father was once more a minister and war was raging in Algeria. Instead of asking to be posted to a quiet French garrison town, as many another minister's son might have done, Claude volunteered for active service and found himself with an artillery regiment at Colomb-Béchar, in the north-western Sahara (25, pp. 43-4). He says little about this period in his autobiographical works, but his friend Pierre Panen points out the difficulties he faced there as the son of a minister and mentions his reactions to 'les effets pervers de la colonisation', the war, the use of torture and the many children suffering from trachoma—a painful eye disease, easily treatable, but which can otherwise lead to blindness (25, p. 45). His stay in war-torn Algeria must at times have given Claude first-hand experience of the kind of fear that some of his fictional characters, including Firmin and Edmond, were to undergo in wartime. It must also have helped him to understand and analyse their reactions on having to go to war. The author, like his two characters, was willing to serve his country but all three were caught up in a process not of their own making with which they had to come to terms. In Firmin's case, this involved cultivating an attitude of appropriate detachment (**52-3**).

When demobilisation came in the autumn of 1960, Claude, now twenty-two, was at last able to take over his farm at Marcillac. It was small; of its nineteen and a half hectares, only eight were cultivable and the soil was not good. But at least he could run it as he wished, applying the methods he had learned at college, to the great scandal of his more traditionally-minded neighbours (*7*, p. 63). The Corrèze, where he and they lived, like the *Causse* in the adjoining Lot where *La Grande Muraille* is set, is a hilly region, in the western beginnings of the Massif Central. Traditional agriculture had remained virtually unchanged there for centuries. It was based on subsistence, with any surplus going to market: each family prided itself on growing corn and grapes to produce their own bread and wine, even though the soil was ill adapted to wheat production and the wine they made was scarcely fit to drink (*7*, p. 63). Tractors were a rarity; it was only at the beginning of the century that the sickle had begun to be replaced by the cutter/binder—drawn by a horse, an ox or often a cow—for harvesting corn. Ploughing was done across, rather than along the contours (a scourge in developing countries to this day), allowing the rain to wash the soil away downhill along the furrows (*7*, p. 42). Hay was cut with scythes—a beautiful spectacle to watch, but exhausting work—and tossed, to help it to dry in the fields, with wooden rakes. This was the pattern of rural life that is portrayed at the beginning of *La Grande Muraille*. Its author was only too well acquainted with it at first hand and was determined henceforth to use his land to better purpose.

Soon after taking over the farm at Marcillac, Claude married Bernadette Delmond, whose family lived at Perpezac-le-Blanc, a village to the north-west of Brive. This was to be the model for the St-Libéral-sur-Diamond of the trilogy which begins with *Des grives aux loups*. When he started transforming Marcillac, he decided to specialise in livestock, so in addition to all the milking there were new pastures to sow and miles of fencing to be put up, an operation which may even have found an unconscious echo in *La Grande Muraille*, as we shall see. Cash flow was a constant problem and there was soon a growing family to feed.

The hero of *Rocheflame,* a novel he was to write later, is also a small farmer, but finds himself in an even worse situation, since his marriage is in danger. Moreover, he too has literary ambitions, which the author describes as 'le délire intégral':

> Il aimait écrire, c'est un vice comme un autre. Peut-être n'aurait-il jamais découvert le plaisir de composer s'il ne s'était tant ennuyé pendant vingt-huit mois sous les drapeaux. Affecté dans un poste perdu sur un piton des Aurès, il eût pu, comme bien d'autres, devenir champion de belote, apprendre par cœur des pages entières de romans pornographiques, sombrer dans la folie douce, contracter un début de cirrhose, ou plus simplement, dépérir d'inaction. La rédaction de contes limousins l'avait occupé plusieurs mois. Un copain, instituteur, s'était chargé du reste. Correcteur bénévole, agent littéraire d'occasion, Michel lui devait la parution de son premier volume. Édité par une modeste maison de province, les historiettes s'étaient taillé un gentil succès local. Depuis, ça n'allait pas très fort... son texte lui semblait tellement bête et plat qu'il donnait ses feuilles à sa femme pour allumer le feu. (*6,* pp. 22-3)

In Claude's case, writing turned out to have its uses. In 1966 he was invited to write the editorial for an agricultural weekly, *Le Moniteur agricole.* This was very welcome, as it brought in some useful additional income (*7,* p. 102; *25,* pp. 61-2) and Claude soon became an agricultural journalist of note: after the *Moniteur* closed down he wrote for *Agrisept,* which later became *Le Nouvel Agriculteur.* The discipline of having to produce four pages of typescript on a different topic every week was not an easy one, but it was an excellent apprenticeship for a writer.

Before embarking on journalism, he had already made his literary début with a novel, *La Terre qui demeure,* printed at the author's expense by *Le Moniteur agricole* in 1965. It is now unobtainable, but Pierre Panen (*25,* p. 77) describes its contents, which presage the subjects of many of the later books: 'la terre, les problèmes paysans, les personnages bien campés durs à la tâche, le modernisme dérangeant, les promoteurs immobiliers avides et rapaces, l'écologie, les successions...' Before that, during the mid-1960s, Claude had written eight or nine novels, three or four of them detective novels set in the countryside and all written with great speed—one of the earliest ones was completed in a fortnight. They were all turned down, so, like his fictional hero, he burned the typescripts and started afresh, concluding from the refusals that the publishers must have had good reasons for turning them down and that he was capable of doing better. An additional motive for burning them was 'pour ne pas avoir la tentation de [se] copier [lui]-même' (*Int*).

Behind all these literary efforts there lay a considerable input in the shape of a lifetime of omnivorous reading. Its pace continues unabated to this day. Among authors that have influenced him particularly he mentions Dickens—read at an early age and re-read—Giono, Malraux (for his power of expression), Mauriac (for his style), the Americans Steinbeck, Caldwell and Faulkner (for their freedom in the use of language) and Bernanos, the latter more for his polemical writings than for his novels (*Int*). If Claude was able to continue reading and writing while running his farm with great efficiency, it was thanks to great self-discipline and to a very organised attitude to the use of time. Such an attitude, can, in some people take on a hectic and selfish character, but Claude Michelet has a gift for putting visitors at their ease and making them feel honoured guests. It is a rare quality.

It was in 1969 that Claude at last found a publisher for what he considers to be his first real novel, *La Grande Muraille*. Since then he has to date published eight more novels, in addition to a number of other successful works, biographical, autobiographical and polemical, these last written in defence of French agriculture and, in particular, of small farmers. His latest novel, *La Nuit de Calama,* appeared in 1994. These works will be briefly discussed in Chapter Five.

Combining the career of a highly successful novelist with that of running a farm, achieved by great self-discipline and by burning the candle at both ends for many years, told on Claude's health. Eventually he had to make the inevitable choice and hand over the working of the farm to others. This has allowed him and his wife, an invaluable companion in literary as in other matters, to devote themselves to writing and to their children and grandchildren. Their grief has been all the greater at the loss of their son, David.

For there is a sad coda to this biographical sketch. The next-to-youngest of the Michelets' six children, David, volunteered during his national service to serve with the French Army's contingent with UNPROFOR, the United Nations peace-keeping force, in Bosnia during the war there. As a direct result of his service he was taken ill, repatriated to France, and died there during the spring of 1995 at the age of twenty-one.

Chapter Two

La Grande Muraille: the novel

La Grande Muraille, which appeared early in 1969, is considered by Claude Michelet to be his first novel although, as we have seen, it had been preceded by La Terre qui demeure and several unpublished attempts at the genre. It was written quickly—over a period of two months during 1968—despite the fact that the writing had to be done at the end of a day's hard work on the farm (Int). The book, published by Julliard with a run of three thousand copies, sold reasonably well, attracted some favourable comment (notably in Le Figaro littéraire and Les Nouvelles littéraires) and formed a good foundation for Claude's subsequent writings, notably for the Saint-Libéral trilogy. It is a good novel in its own right. Its plot is a simple one, recounting the life of Firmin Malpeyre. Both of the hero's names are significant. The first echoes the idea of standing firm against adversity: St Firmin, who became bishop of Amiens, was born in Pamplona, in Northern Spain, where bulls still run through the streets each year to celebrate his feast-day. The second is the name of a village a dozen kilometres south of Brive. Its French meaning, 'mauvaise pierre', evokes with suitable irony the nature of Firmin's inheritance. Claude Michelet chose these names, as he does others, both personal and topographical, with care. He often uses local place names in his novels, though not necessarily in their usual locations. Family names are also typically local ones, as a glance at the Brive telephone directory will show, and personal ones match both locality and period (Int). A particular example is the family name 'Vialhe' from the Saint-Libéral trilogy, which was based on the maiden name of Claude's mother, Marie Vialle.

Summary

Firmin is a twenty-five-year-old farm worker living in a *bourg* (a large village where markets are held) in the Corrèze in July 1914. When he was five, his father had been crushed to death when a cart lost a wheel and its load of timber fell on him. His ailing mother had died of tuberculosis soon afterwards, so his father's brother, Alfred, and his wife, Berthe, had taken Firmin in and brought him up with their own two sons, Émile and Edmond, and their daughter, Léonie. Firmin had not fitted easily into their family. The spirit of revolt which took his uncle and aunt as its main target was really the unconscious expression of his anger and resentment at having lost his parents, but they saw it only as base ingratitude on his part. The mutual hostility which developed between Firmin and his uncle persisted when the boy grew into manhood.

The whole village is amazed, therefore, when Alfred dies and leaves a piece of land to Firmin. The amazement turns to amusement when it becomes clear that the field, le Bois des Roches, is covered in a deep layer of stones. The *curé* sees this cruel and malicious practical joke for what it is. Firmin, however, on exploring the field, discovers that the soil is fertile beneath the stones and starts to clear them, to the general mockery—which his uncle intended—of the village. These events, however, are soon interrupted by the outbreak of the First World War. On the assassination of Archduke Ferdinand, the heir to the Austrian throne, in Sarajevo, Austria has declared war on Serbia, whose ally, Russia, comes to its defence. Soon Germany, France and Britain are involved, as is most of Europe. Firmin survives the battle of the Marne and is joined near Verdun, the scene of the fiercest battles of the whole war, by his cousin, Edmond, whom he had looked down on as being much too pious when they were boys but had since learned to respect. The two spend the rest of the war together and come out of it scarred by wounds but with decorations for bravery. Émile, however, is killed. As for Léonie, having flirted with Firmin before the war, she marries a rich man whose varicose veins—and perhaps *piston* or underhand influence—have saved him from being called up.

Edmond completes his training for the priesthood and Firmin returns to his stony field, knowing now what he wants to do, which is to build, with the stones from his field, a wall which will both serve as a boundary and be a thing of beauty, in his eyes at least. The people of the village, however, mock his efforts still more and treat him as mad, so that as his wall gradually gains height, he himself becomes more and more isolated. He even loses the only real friend he had in the village when the old *curé* dies. Hope is renewed, however, when the new *curé* turns out to be Edmond, who immediately sets out to try to reintegrate Firmin into village life.

The inter-war years go by, with their succession of national and international events, and by the time of the Second World War, with the *débâcle* of 1940 and the Occupation, the wall is of impressive proportions, having a garden on top and alcoves built into it for storage. Edmond joins the Resistance and provokes Firmin's fury when he uses the wall to store explosives, but Firmin supports Edmond's efforts in his own way and treats the local collaborators with contempt. He fools a party of Germans foraging for food, and when a party of ill-disciplined *maquisards* want to use his wall to execute an informer, he sends them packing. Despite Firmin's declared anticlericalism, Edmond persuades him to take the place of his old sacristan and when D-Day comes he rings the bells so loudly, despite the Mayor's protests, that one of them cracks.

By the end of the war Firmin's wall is complete on one side of the field and he decides to start on the next section. Although he is still thought of in the village as being mad, the old viciousness has gone and people are somewhat more tolerant. He realises one day, however, that he is getting older and that the work is going much more slowly. The idea makes him deeply depressed and he stops work, but Edmond reassures him and he returns to the task of completing the wall, which henceforth becomes a virtual obsession. After another ten years the second section has reached the respectable height of one metre—the main wall, in contrast, is three metres high. Firmin makes a start on the next layer of stones but a fortnight later he has a heart attack while he is serving Mass for Edmond. As Edmond gives him the last sacraments, Firmin wonders whether he has wasted his whole life on a useless project. Edmond, however, assures him that everything has a use and, at Firmin's request, promises to bless his wall. Firmin still wonders why he had built the wall, but the whole idea now seems to him to be amusing and as he draws his last breath he has a smile on his face.

Sources and genesis

Some possible parallels to this unusual story about a man taking on a colossal task could be sought in Claude Michelet's own situation when he wrote it. At the time, the joy of having his own farm must at times have been at least partly overshadowed by the difficulty of the tasks he faced. The memory of the many kilometres of barbed wire and other fencing he had had to put up so as to keep his animals in could well have evoked, if only unconsciously, the idea of an almost endless task comparable to that of constructing a Great Wall (*7*, p. 93). Indeed, the routine of farming life can seem endless, especially that of milking: I have never forgotten the French small farmer I met who was able to take his first holiday in forty years when he sold his last cow. Yet to one who loves farming and had fought to become a farmer, such chores must have been what weighed least. Harder, perhaps, was trying to make a living for a growing family in the face of all kinds of obstacles: natural ones such as drought, frost and flood; financial ones such as getting only poor prices, as the small farmer often does, for his produce whilst having to pay high ones for machinery, fertiliser and seeds. Yet the greatest source of discouragement was perhaps the feeling that his problems and the long-term importance for the country of small farmers like him were not appreciated by those in power in Paris and Brussels. The strains which such worries could impose on those concerned are well illustrated, as we shall see later, in his next novel, *Rocheflame*.

Although the problems of the small farmer's life almost certainly lie behind the composition of *La Grande Muraille,* composing it must also have constituted an escape from them. Its immediate inspiration, however, was a very solid one, for the wall itself exists. One of the many attractions of the Brive area, ten kilometres to the south-west of the town, is an artificial lake called the Lac du Causse, which is used for swimming and water sports. About five kilometres further south is the village of Chartrier-Ferrière and at the western end of the village a track on the northern side of the D154 road leads down to the remarkable construction on which *La Grande Muraille* is modelled; there is in fact a photograph of it on the cover of the standard Laffont edition. (The map reference is given in the bibliography.) It is smaller than Firmin's wall, with only one section, just under seventy metres long—Firmin's has two, the first, built to full height, a hundred metres long and the second one metre high and eighty-five long (**117**). Like Firmin's main wall, however, the Chartrier wall is about three metres high, is very solidly constructed—some of the stones at the base must weigh well over a quarter of a ton—and had a garden on top of the broadest end, at which point it is about four metres wide. One can still see the remains of a vine growing up the wall and it has alcoves which are still there, half way along, though not as elaborately constructed as Firmin's. It is now fairly easy of access, but when Claude Michelet first came across it, by chance, in the 1960s, it was in the middle of the woods, and a much more surprising sight to come upon, with its hanging garden, its vine and traces of paving around the vegetable patches of the garden (*Int*). A notice at one end, with a plan and details of the dimensions, explains how it came to be built:

LA GRANDE MURAILLE

Mur en pierre sèche construit par M. Faurel Louis,
de 1934 à 1948, date de sa mort, pour pouvoir
cultiver son champ, planter sa vigne
et délimiter sa parcelle.

Sur sa muraille il a aménagé un jardin et un trou
pour ranger ses outils. Il avait prévu une citerne
et une étable pour son âne. À la base du mur,
on voit des terriers pour les lapins.

It also says that the builder's daughter, Mme Magnan, of the 'bourg de Chartrier' will show visitors around the wall, 'dont Claude Michelet a raconté l'histoire dans un de ses livres.'

It is not, of course, the story of M. Faurel's wall that is told in *La Grande Muraille,* although it did serve as the initial inspiration for the book. In fact, on seeing the wall, the author realised that he had to choose between writing a biography of its real-life builder and leaving it to his own imagination to solve the mystery of its construction. Fortunately for us he chose the latter course. Indeed he deliberately made no inquiries about the origins of the real wall until the novel was completed. He also changed the wall's location. Chartrier is in the Corrèze, but in the beginnings of the *Causse,* a term which defines both a local area and a type of country characterised by hills with abundant limestone outcrops and stone walls rather like those of the Pennines or the Yorkshire Dales, which serve both to clear the fields of stones and to keep in the flocks. Claude Michelet decided to place Firmin's wall and his imaginary village, Les Landes, in the heart of the *Causse,* further south in the *département* of the Lot (*Int*).

Structure and language

As we have seen, the plot of *La Grande Muraille* is a simple one, tracing one man's life from 1914 to its end in 1956, but the story

line is firm and in its own way foreshadows the more complex ones
of the later works. As with Michelet's other novels, the book is set in
a precise historical context, but as it is centred on the rather unusual
life of Firmin, the only events which stand out, since they impinge
directly on his existence, are the two world wars. For many years
after 1918, the world passes him by. Then Edmond buys a radio and
from 1936 onwards he takes an interest in outside events until the
final race with time to complete the second part of the wall (**153**). I
have suggested in an article (*24*, p. 31) that one cannot really see *La
Grande Muraille* as a historical novel, certainly not in the same way
as the Saint-Libéral novels or the Chilean trilogy, since it is
concerned mainly with characters, notably those of Firmin and
Edmond. It does, however, convey some of the period atmosphere
that characterises the later novels. We see something of the
flourishing rural life of pre-1914 France, together with its sectarian
squabbles, the attitudes of villagers to each other and the chauvinist
enthusiasm which was widespread at the outbreak of war. We also
see the harsh realities of that war and are given a vivid feeling of
what it was like to be present at the battle of Verdun (**69-72**). We
are shown the impact at local level of the terrible slaughter,
something that we can usually sense only by reading through the long
lists of dead on the war memorials when visiting French villages.
Later, at the time of the Second World War, we are made to feel the
atmosphere of Les Landes during the Occupation, with some
villagers supporting and others opposing Vichy (**126-8**) and learn
that as well as the well-disciplined *maquisards,* there were those who
behaved more like thugs and who, in the book at least, paid the price
(**130-33**). As has been noted, the author was well informed about
the events he describes in both World Wars and had direct personal
experience of the Second.

 La Grande Muraille is simply structured, following a linear
pattern from Firmin's inheriting of his field to his death thirty-eight
years later, with brief references back to his childhood and earlier
life in the first chapter. The first five chapters take us to the end of
the 1914-1918 War, the next three cover the inter-war years and the
final three the 1939-1945 War and its aftermath. The book is written
in the third person, with the author in control of the narration,
usually recounting the characters' thoughts as well as their words and
actions, but with occasional use of free indirect speech, as when the
expression of Firmin's early thoughts about his new legacy moves
from the first to the third person (**11**). Also, as was to happen in the

later novels (and in particular with the Chilean trilogy—see Chapter
Five), the ideas and values that the characters express are their own;
we are left to draw our own conclusions about them, rather than
having the author's views imposed on us. The conclusions to be
drawn about Émile from his pejorative remarks about Firmin, for
instance (25), are fairly obvious, but the author does not take sides
between the ideological views of the cleric (but not 'clerical')
Edmond and those of the anticlerical Firmin and he notably leaves
open the question of the reasons for, and the value of, Firmin's
building his wall; an element of ambiguity persists throughout.

Paradoxical as it may seem in the context of a book about a man
who is at one time reduced to talking to himself, the use of dialogue
is a striking feature of *La Grande Muraille*. Indeed the dialogue is
well observed and often colourful, whether it is a laconic
conversation in the midst of a battle where Firmin, Edmond and a
corporal are in a desperate predicament (70-72) or a row between
Firmin and the Pétain supporters in the bistrot over the Marshal's
portrait (126). Most of the dialogue, in fact, consists of the everyday
speech of a village in an out-of-the-way part of southern France.
Claude Michelet was well placed to know the speech of Firmin and
his generation. He writes his dialogue in French, but manages to
convey the feel of the Limousin dialect which was the normal speech
of the villages of that part of France in their day. The *achevez
d'entrer* which invites visitors to come in is a literal translation of
acabatz d'entrar and Firmin's oaths: *vingtdiou, miladiou,* are, of
course, pure Limousin.

The question of regional languages (often disparagingly referred
to as 'patois', a word which strictly speaking implies a local,
degenerate version of a dialect, which in turn is the regional version
of a language), together with the question of regional identity, is
very much a subject of dispute in certain parts of France, and
particularly in the Midi. Limousin is a dialect of the *langue d'oc* (*oc*
is the equivalent of the French *oui*), which is a completely separate
language from French. Its ancestor, Old Provençal, was once the
leading literary language of medieval Europe. Although French, for
political reasons, gradually supplanted it on both the administrative
and the literary planes, its successor dialects were spoken widely
throughout southern France until quite recently and they still
survive. There was a modern literary revival, which reached a peak
in the nineteenth century. It was led by Frédéric Mistral, who lived
near Avignon, and over the years has produced some fine works, as

well as much 'folklore fodder'. However, the pressure exerted by the schools (where regional languages used to be persecuted) and of the media, together with the rural exodus, has gravely reduced the currency of the language. The centre of gravity of the revival has moved from Provence itself to Toulouse, and the language now tends to be known as Occitan (from *oc*). Claude Michelet's mother-tongue being French, he of course writes in French, but, although he has kept aside from the Occitan movement, he is well acquainted with its language.

Descriptions

La Grande Muraille is not particularly rich in descriptions, in the sense of purple passages. Some scenes, however, are strikingly depicted, such as the village in the early morning (**31**) or the hot summer afternoon on the *Causse,* the plateau to the south of Brive where the rocky bones of the limestone stick out of the grassy hillsides (**10**). Michelet's sense of observation is acute: the senses of sight, smell and touch are brought to bear through the selection of details which build up his picture: the intense light, which hurts the eyes; the dusty smells of hay and earth which, by implication, irritate the nostrils; the heat haze and the brackish water that is all that remains in the storage tanks. He also has a gift for the telling phrase; the 'sèches brebis', shaking off the flies in the heat while the human inhabitants of the *Causse* snooze in 'une sieste moite', a well-chosen transferred epithet—an unusual stylistic device in French— conveying here an image of the perspiring sleepers (**10**). Elsewhere an apparently pedantic reference to 'des graminées ligneuses' conveys perfectly the very coarse grass that alone could survive in such an environment (**20**). Similarly the mention of 'une demi-cartonnée d'avoine' (**23**) may puzzle the uninitiated but is a perfectly natural measure of surface area for a countryman from the Lot.

Images are not frequent but are all the more telling when used, as when Firmin, suddenly inserted into his uncle's family, is compared to 'une feuille volante entre les pages d'un livre bien relié' (**12-13**)—it sticks out all the more from the rest. The descriptions of Firmin's stony field give rise to more images, such as those of the twisted bushes in this 'lac minéral' which 'semblaient se nourrir de pierres' (**20**) and of the root which Firmin frees from 'l'étau calcaire qui la torturait' (**22**).

Some descriptions paint a physical portrait of a character, as does that of Firmin, a striking figure, tall, well-made and handsome with his blue eyes and his fair moustache—hair tends to be dark in southern France (9); so do Firmin's comments on the stooped figure of Émile (37). These physical descriptions are necessary, since they differentiate between the two characters: Firmin is upright both physically and morally while Émile is bowed down under the burden of his materialism. Yet we are given no detailed picture of Edmond, apart from the fact that he wears a black cassock. We do not need one; his behaviour is what matters and it speaks for itself.

It is via details, visual or aural, that we are given a picture of life in the village in its heyday before the First World War: the hungry and excited hens which 'attendaient fébrilement le grain', the sounds of animals calling and of scythes being sharpened in the early morning description already quoted (31). This last example and that of the rows of hay that Firmin cuts for the Chastaing family (16) remind us that the scythe was the usual tool used at that time for cutting hay—machinery was rare. Similarly the mere fact that Firmin is the village barber makes us realise that the village did not need a full-time one. It did, however, have a solicitor then, and his status in relation to the ordinary villagers is shown in the little cameo of the scene in which he opens Alfred's will, savouring every moment of the mini-drama which he acts out (8-9). The practice of mutual assistance at busy times, which then prevailed and was indeed essential in the absence of machinery, is illustrated by Firmin's being invited to help on both the Chastaing and the Delfour farms (16). In the event he refuses both and prefers to explore his inheritance.

Again, the wild patriotic fervour that gripped France on the outbreak of war in 1914 is well shown by the scenes in the village: the defeat of France by Germany in 1870 was now at last going to be avenged and Alsace-Lorraine recaptured. Similar scenes of young men departing to the sound of the *Marseillaise,* with the women weeping in the background (50-51), must have been repeated in villages all over the land. So must the scene Firmin finds when he goes back to Les Landes on leave in 1915, with the bereaved suffering silently in their misery while the rest, the old, the genuinely sick and unfit for service and the well-connected draft-dodgers, 'les malades et les présumés tels, les réformés définitifs et les réformés par relations' (61) enjoyed their good fortune at not being called up; the front was in every sense a long way away for those who did not have to fight. Significant detail lends atmosphere and authenticity to both scenes; in the first one, père Laroche (the title marks him as the eldest man in his family) dispenses strong drink and lurid advice ('coupez-les-leur'—**51**) to the departing conscripts while, in the more sombre second one, Firmin deliberately waits till the last day of his leave before visiting Edmond's mother so he can be sure that her son is still alive.

The author's descriptions of the war in the trenches have a sense of immediacy thanks to his sense of observation and his knowledge both of the subject and of human beings. The chilling realities of hand-to-hand fighting with knives and sharpened spades (**67**); the deadly effect when a shell hits a tree and hurls its steel splinters through the air rather than into soft ground (**69**); Firmin's failure to reply to Edmond's letters because there was nothing to tell him that he did not already know (**72**), then Firmin's vain efforts to forget the war after it was over (**73**)—all these ring true. Similar scenes convey the atmosphere of the Occupation and the divisions it provoked in French society: Firmin's comments on Pétain's portrait in the bistrot and the ensuing quarrel (**126**); Edmond's secret radio, hidden in the church belltower (**129-30**); the episode of the *maquisards* (**130-33**); the German foraging party (**133-7**); Firmin's taunting of the mayor when the news of the Allied landings comes (**142-3**). Many of them, as we have seen, are based on the author's own experiences or those of his father. Claude Michelet's descriptions throughout the book give the reader a sense of presence which is raised to a heightened degree in the later novels—to choose but one example, in the terrifying account of the storming of the Peruvian fortress of Arica by the Chilean army in *Pour un arpent de terre* (*12*, pp. 376-8). Descriptions, then, are well conveyed in *La Grande Muraille,* but the main source of interest lies less in descriptions than in the treatment of character.

Chapter Three

La Grande Muraille: characters

The primacy accorded to character over incident and description in *La Grande Muraille,* although the latter are well conveyed, lends the whole book a kind of classical simplicity. As in a Racine play, rather than the events themselves, it is the characters and the way in which they react to them that hold our attention. This concentration on the study of human behaviour is at the heart of the great French literary tradition to which Claude Michelet can justly claim to belong.

The villagers

In discussing the characters of *La Grande Muraille*, the village of Les Landes itself, as an entity, ought perhaps to be given first consideration. In general, its collective personality is not a very likeable one when seen from Firmin's point of view. Certainly Firmin enjoys the company of some of his neighbours, such as the Chastaing family, 'de braves gens' (**16**), and others are at least amusing in their own way, such as old Laroche, already mentioned, and the Delfour daughter, more gifted with sexual urge than with good looks and always in hot and unscrupulous pursuit of a suitable husband: 'même pas avec un sac sur la tête!' sums up Firmin's unwillingness to oblige (**17**). But the great majority of the villagers are narrow-minded and intolerant and it needs but little for them to become actively hostile, as Firmin knows only too well and to his cost. Intolerance and hostility in French villages, incidentally, are not confined to the pages of fiction; real-life examples are to be found, for instance, in *Une soupe aux herbes sauvages* (*27*), the autobiography of Émilie Carles, who was a country schoolmistress in the 1930s. No doubt parallel examples are to be found in other countries, including our own.

At the forefront of all this in Les Landes are the gossips, the 'bonnes langues', mostly female, as the opening of the book shows (though as we shall see, Émile is no slouch). Appearances are all-important for them and the shirt-tail hanging from Firmin's trousers as he goes to the solicitor's office confirms all their worst prejudices and damns him even more in their eyes (**8**). Later, when he decides to 'reprendre sa sieste interrompue', we realise that he had, in fact, only just got out of bed (**15**); this shows not only that he is a typical feckless bachelor but also that he is neither nosy nor materialistic, unlike the women. Their necks crane forward behind their curtains when he enters the office, as though, even at that distance, they might be able to hear what was being said. The ill will of some of them can be quite vicious, as in their suggestion that it was the strain of his uncle's recent quarrel with Firmin that had killed him, even though everyone knew that he had died of a stomach complaint (**8**). A similar calumny, in *Des grives aux loups,* is at least partially responsible for the suicide of the father of young Léon, who at thirteen is left with the responsibility of looking after his mother and young sister. Years later, it is the gossips of Les Landes who cause the old *curé* to die alone when his housekeeper goes out for 'un brin de causette' (**96-7**); Firmin's anger is very understandable.

Alfred and Berthe

The basic values of most of the other village people, or at least the values they appear to practise, seem very different from those of Firmin and Edmond, which we shall examine later. We are told, for instance, that Edmond's parents, Alfred and Berthe, 'n'étaient pas méchants. Sans doute même étaient-ils bons' (**13**). They took young Firmin into their own family when he was orphaned—no small act of generosity—but not understanding how profoundly and in what ways bereavement can affect a child, they were completely taken aback when he seemed to be turning against them in what was really a revolt against his fate. Certainly Firmin must have been a handful, and one can but sympathise with their plight. Moreover his reaction to their gesture looked to them like base ingratitude, but Alfred, 'un peu brutal et sévère' (**13**), cannot have been easy to live with for a boy who, as the only son, had probably been accustomed to gentler ways. Worst of all, the family naggingly insist on their own virtuousness and clearly always have done—Berthe's automatic 'Nous t'avons élevé comme un fils', echoing Émile's reproach, triggers an equally automatic reply from Firmin: 'Je sais, c'est pas nouveau' (**10**). This kind of reaction must have stifled long since any latent feeling of gratitude he may once have had towards them and time had clearly done nothing to heal the wounds.

Alfred's attempt at revenge via his will may, then, seem to have some justification. Firmin's first reaction is to dismiss it as 'une joyeuse blague' (11)—he himself inflicts funny haircuts in a joking spirit on those who mock him—and he takes no offence at his uncle's gesture. One might therefore suppose that the village, having laughed and talked about the matter for a time, would then forget it. But the *curé*, knowing Firmin's independent nature and the sensitivity that lay beneath an apparently bluff exterior, is surely right in seeing Alfred's gesture as 'une méchanceté' (18). This is confirmed by Berthe's insistence, when talking to her children, that her husband had not left the field to Firmin simply for Émile to buy it back from him; that would have allowed the affair to blow over too quickly. Clearly, there was nastiness in Alfred's gesture and Berthe subscribes to it—'ton père a bien fait'. Émile echoes it, too, in his verdict: 'Firmin, c'est de la mauvaise graine'. Only Edmond springs to his defence (25). In fact, with the sole exception of Edmond, meanness of spirit seems to be a dominating characteristic of the whole family. Certainly it is not conducive to a happy life on their part. Berthe, 'déjà aigrie' when Firmin joined the family (13), seems to find fault in other people every time she speaks. When Firmin returns to the village having survived the war, we find the *curé* delicately, but unnecessarily, given Firmin's tactfulness, having to hint to him that he should not visit Berthe, whose elder son, Émile, had been killed (79). A more normal and less embittered person than Berthe might rather have sent for Firmin to thank him for saving the life of her younger son, Edmond, by carrying him to safety under fire (72).

Émile and Léonie

Émile's life was no less miserable. His totally negative remarks about Firmin are symptomatic, as is his inveterate bad temper. He looks older than he is. At twenty-eight, his facial expression, 'déjà épaisse, était ridée, butée'; besides his furrowed brow, he was acquiring a stoop. Firmin's diagnoses materialism, but expresses it more bluntly: 'peut-être c'est sa femme qui le crève, mais peut-être aussi c'est de compter les sous qu'elle lui a apportés...' (37).

The pretty Léonie at first seems a more attractive person, and Firmin has a soft spot for her, even seeing her as a possible wife

(14), but in her eyes Firmin has no more than entertainment value. Her mother has no need to warn her against assignations with him; she is fully conscious of the most important factor: 'il n'avait pas de quoi nourrir une femme!' (26). Léonie's silence when Émile is attacking Firmin's character during this same conversation is perhaps understandable, since she is in danger of being compromised. But when she visits him in his field and Émile comes up offering to buy it, her quiet disappearance, 'sans mot dire et sans bruit' (38), is not motivated by fear of reproach from Émile. It is the result of a calculated decision to break off all contact with someone who is not 'un homme normal' (34) and Firmin finds it particularly hurtful to be treated by her as 'un innocent'—a village idiot (43).

They next meet when Firmin is on leave during the war. Léonie deliberately seeks him out in his field, where he has gone to work in peace for a few days, but it is not to enquire after his health or that of Edmond. She has come specially to tell him that she is getting married. Her future husband is rich, and besides being thirty-eight— twice her age—is exempt from call-up because of varicose veins. Firmin, to her fury, hints at the connection between her fiancé's income and the medical diagnosis (63). He realises that her sole aim in coming to see him is to try and make him jealous, and he foresees her taking lovers as her husband gets older; her sole concern is for herself. She gets her well-merited come-uppance in Firmin's crisp parting shot, being assured that when he returns to the front he will give her love to Edmond, whose name she had not mentioned (64).

The old *curé*

One turns with relief to a more sympathetic character, the old *curé*. He is all the more sympathetic since he belongs to a generation of the clergy that had lived through the bitterest days of anticlericalism, which was at its height in the years before the First World War. As we have seen, the comradeship of the trenches was to reduce its violence and lead to the setting up after the war of movements such as the *Équipes sociales,* so dear to the heart of Edmond Michelet. Although the tone of Les Landes was fiercely republican (7), the *curé* has clearly been able to prevent political differences from turning into personal ones and he genuinely cares for all the people of the village. Firmin teases him with anticlerical banter (e.g. 17), but it is good-hearted and he is never lacking in proper respect towards him. One is led to think that the *curé* had always kept a discreet eye on the welfare of the young orphan.

Whether or not that is true, the *curé,* no longer young himself in 1914, is the only person in the village, apart from Edmond, to show any concern for Firmin. He sees Alfred's perfidious legacy for what it is and tries to help Firmin to examine his motives for embarking on his project, but without condemning him in the way that everyone else does. The comparison he makes with the Tower of Babel leaves Firmin puzzled—clearly he was a reluctant attender at Sunday catechism classes—but the underlying idea that he may be defying the world and trying to prove something to himself or others strikes home **(41)**. The two next meet on Firmin's return from the war; the *curé* is the only person then to offer him 'le verre du retour' **(78)**. He also shows himself still concerned for the young man's future. Firmin has now decided that he is going to build his wall, but assures the old man that he has no wish to 'défier le monde' and that if he is mad he is less so than a world which makes war. The *curé* concurs and drinks to Firmin's work **(79-80)**, thus according it a dignity which no one else, save Edmond, is willing to grant and, as it were, anticipating the blessing which his cousin promises on its completion.

The relationship between the two men is an unusual and paradoxical one, given Firmin's outspoken anticlericalism, but both know that there is no malice in the latter, in contrast with much of the village gossip. The *curé* clearly appreciates Firmin's tact and understanding in not visiting his aunt on his return from the war; these must have been rare qualities in the village. Later, when the old man dies, neglected by women who no doubt see themselves as pillars of the Church and models of Christian charity, the anticlerical Firmin is the only man in the village to follow his coffin. This was a gesture not to be underestimated in those times—the other men would have been afraid of being ridiculed as churchgoers had they followed Firmin's example, the funeral of a parish priest being usually a large and public affair, attended by all the neighbouring clergy. Even more touching is the last humble service which Firmin renders the *curé:* he pays the gravedigger to let him fill in the grave, a gesture seen in the village as a further sign of his madness **(98)**.

Firmin

The anticlerical Firmin is certainly paradoxical in that his only two friends are priests. As he says to Edmond, 'Moi, je ne suis pas

calotin et c'est rien qu'avec des curés que je peux causer' (**87**). The
early loss of both parents might have turned anyone else into a
permanent rebel against God. Firmin certainly turns into a rebel, but
as he is not of a metaphysical turn of mind his rebellion is directed
against a closer target, his uncle and aunt. We have noted their
constant reminders to him of their own generosity, which make them
perhaps not totally undeserving of his anger, while Émile, older and
always smugly rubbing in the fact that Firmin has neither parents
nor property, must have seemed equally unendearing to him (**13**).
Firmin's obsession with independence is thus totally understandable
in the circumstances. Yet however smug and uncharitable Émile's
jibes may be, they are unfortunately based on fact. All that his
parents had managed to leave Firmin was his little house and its
garden. He has no source of income in the form of land. Fortunately
his needs are few; his garden keeps him in food and he can earn what
little cash he needs by acting as village barber and by working for
neighbours. But all this would change if he were to think of getting
married, as Léonie knows only too well. His treasured independence
would disappear overnight and he would have to go cap in hand in
search of whatever work he could find.

The situation, however, never arises, because his uncle's legacy
changes everything for him. He is then faced with the choice of
either leaving the field as it is, thereby both publicly admitting defeat
in his long battle with his uncle and confirming the latter's judgment
of him as a nonentity—'on lui offrait son complément' (**11**)—or else
of taking on the impossible task of trying to do something about it.
After his first visit to the field he decides to take up the challenge: 'Je
vais leur faire voir moi...' but at the same time he realises that to try
and do so would be madness (the word, taken up by others, appears
first in his own thoughts): though 'insensé', it would also be
'merveilleux', since he would be acting of his own free will (**29**). At
this point, the shadow of his twenty-year battle with Alfred for
independence looms large in his thinking. (There are, incidentally,
possible parallels here with the struggles of Jean-Édouard's children
to break free of their father's domination in the later novel *Des
grives aux loups* and also, unconsciously perhaps, with Claude
Michelet's own battle, with a much more understanding father, to be
allowed to go to agricultural school.) The independence which
Firmin has fought for and won dominates his whole life. Even when
he is in the army, where he accepts military discipline because he has
to, he still defies orders and persuades Edmond, virtually by moral

blackmail, to join his crow-hunting escapade. It earns them a medal each, but, as Edmond points out, it could just as easily have led to their being killed or court-martialled (**55-61**).

Firmin's taking on of his task both guarantees his treasured independence and solves his economic problems, in the sense that when he returns from the war and sets to work, his needs are as simple as they ever were. There is, however, a price to pay. Firstly, people think he is mad and treat him as such. Secondly, he now understands that marriage is not possible for him, for, as he tells the *curé*, no girl would have him: 'J'en trouverai pas une assez folle...' The nature of his work would make her laugh at him (**80**). It would obviously also leave him no time for earning money to keep the family that later, when on his deathbed, he laments at not having had (**157**). His life is thus perforce a life of celibacy, although not, to the *curé*'s regret, one of chastity (**80**).

To sum up, Firmin's aims in first undertaking his task are twofold: firstly, to take up his uncle's challenge and secondly, to do a job of his own choosing, a job which preserves his independence. For him, his little domain is at once the sign and the symbol of that independence. In return, however, he has to sacrifice everything else to it. He recognises that the idea of clearing his field is crazy, but it gives him what he is seeking, a job of his own choosing: '...c'est idiot, oui mais [...] c'est du travail au moins...' (**30**) and it is 'le travail d'un homme libre' (**29**). This, moreover, is an idea which he frequently repeats (e.g. **34**; **41**; **93**). The village, however, immediately reacts to him with mockery. Initially, as we have seen, he responds to this in his function as barber by giving some of the mockers funny haircuts, notably tonsures, the priest's shaven crown which was the ultimate humiliation in anticlerical company (**42**). But when he returns from the army to a village already embittered by war, the atmosphere is harsher and he is looked down on as the village idiot when he returns to his field (**82**). Yet Edmond, on a visit soon after the war, expresses genuine enthusiasm ('s'extasia') at his progress: 'Tu en as fait un boulot!' and approval: 'c'est le travail que tu t'es choisi, il est bon que tu le finisses' (**84-5**). When he talks then to Firmin about the latter's isolation, Firmin accepts some of the blame for it; he had, for instance, refused to take his rightful place and carry the flag at the 11 November ceremony for fear of mockery, but he insists that it is the villagers who are rejecting him, not the opposite. When he asks Firmin the reason for this, Edmond diagnoses what amounts to a 'Catch-22' situation: the villagers are afraid that Firmin may succeed in his enterprise and thus prove them wrong, so they mock him for what he is doing; if he stopped doing it, however, they would still mock him, this time for giving up (**86**).

Edmond hopes that time will solve the problem, but it does not do so. A few years later, Firmin, now reduced to talking to himself, analyses his situation. He begins with remarkable lucidity, presenting both sides of the problem: on the one hand, the miserable life he leads and his isolation from society; on the other, the need he feels to carry on with his work: 'j'ai besoin de faire ça pour vivre.' (He is, of course, talking here about a way of life, not of earning a living.) He may be lonely, but he argues that unlike others, he can stand it: 'C'est vrai, je suis seul, mais je peux l'être. Si les autres se groupent, c'est parce qu'ils ont peur. [...] Alors ils se groupent comme des moutons...'. They hide their fear, but are lost 'dès qu'ils sont seuls en face d'elle [leur peur]' (**94**).

A sentence, omitted in the printed editions, makes the logic of the passage clearer: 'Ils ne savent se défendre seuls' (*Int*). The printed text then resumes: 'Moi, si!' (**94**) As he continues, however, it begins to sound as though the old *curé*'s first analysis may have been right and that Firmin, like the builders of the Tower of Babel, is either guilty of hubris, overweening pride, or suffering from paranoia: 'ma muraille sera faite et restera debout pendant des siècles...' But his reaction is surely understandable in the light of the circumstances, particularly given his independent nature. He ends up denying that he is mad: 'Non, je ne suis pas fou, je fais ce que je dois faire et j'y trouve ma vie, ça me suffit' (**94**). At this stage of his existence the element of pride and defiance, as evidenced by the first of these two quotations, looms far more largely than it will do later on; the idea expressed by the second, a kind of categorical imperative—I must do what I must do—is one that will persist throughout his life. The whole episode is an attempt by Firmin to overcome an attack of depression and to strengthen his resolve. Signifantly, that day 'resta gravé en lui comme un des plus durs, un des plus pénibles' (**94**). Only when night came did he find peace again—and his work had made some progress.

Firmin may on that occasion have strengthened his resolve, although his isolation subsequently grows ever greater, as is evidenced by the events surrounding the old *curé*'s death. Yet the hurt and anger he feels deep down in spite of his delarations of independence finally break out when Edmond calls to tell him that he is the new parish priest. This gives Firmin the opportunity to open his heart to his cousin: 'Ils me laisseraient crever sans me dire un mot...'. There is, however, no lasting self-pity in him, for he soon smiles and changes the subject (**100**), because Edmond's arrival will bring some warmth and friendship into his life. It also gives him an ally in the village. From then on, matters improve for him: he is still treated as a *fada* (a 'nutter' in the parlance of the Midi), but from now on he is seen as being more an eccentric than a lunatic, and people are prepared to exchange the odd word with him, especially when he gives them fruit from his orchard (**111**).

Firmin's personal character is an admirable one. Although he is a handsome man, he is without vanity (**15**). He has a cheerful disposition and before his isolation he is always joking and making people laugh (e.g. **17**). He gets on well with his neighbours (**16**) and is a great success with the girls (e.g. **19**). He displays considerable courage, both on the battlefield and in standing up to his fellow villagers, and he is certainly not afraid of hard work. He displays high seriousness in his attitude to war, both as the first one starts (**46**) and with the young *maquisards* in the second (**132**). Moreover he has high moral standards—if one sets aside his visits to the ladies of the town (**105**)—and he shows more respect for proper behaviour and decency in both church and civic matters than do the old women who chatter at the old *curé*'s wake after letting him die alone (**96**) or the turncoat mayor who raises his voice in church when Firmin rings the bells to announce D-Day (**142-3**). The mayor in a sense gets the same treatment as the altar boys who fool about behind Edmond's back (**108**). He deserves it, too, because his spinelessness and greed offend Firmin's sense of what is right and proper. When the old *curé* is teased, both know that Firmin means no disrespect (**17-18**); not so with the mayor and his cronies.

Humour, largely centred around Firmin, is in fact a notable feature of *La Grande Muraille*. Despite the miseries inflicted on him, Firmin is basically a cheery soul, as has been said, and is the centre of many amusing incidents. His 'côté goguenard' (**111**), a side of Firmin's independent nature which does not endear him to everyone, is an important aspect of his character and leads him to tease people, but he does not indulge in gratuitous humiliation. His suggestion to the old *curé* that he gets a bonus for each recruit he sends to the seminary (**17**), for instance, is a good-humoured leg-pull and is taken as such, as are many similar mock anticlerical remarks made to Edmond, including the dramatically ironic one made in the heat of battle about becoming a sacristan (**71**). Firmin's humour is very much in the Midi tradition of the *galéjade,* teasing people or 'having them on' by telling tall stories that they may or may not believe. He is also a great prankster, as is illustrated by the wartime crow episode, already noted. This brings a practical return, as does another of his ideas, the cowpat collection service (**89**), the funny side of which he must surely see despite the jokes made at his expense. The comic haircuts he carries out are another of his pranks, but we have already seen that such treatment is inflicted on people who deserve it (**42-3**), such as the German foragers who come to requisition food (**133-7**). His annihilation of the mayor when ringing the bells for D-Day comes into the same category (**142-3**).

Unlike the Mayor and his cronies and unlike his own stepfamily—Edmond, of course, excepted—Firmin is neither greedy nor materialistic; he makes a little income from selling truffles when his little property is well established but he is happy to give away fruit from his garden to those who have allowed him to collect cowpats from their land (**91**) and he leaves the honey in his hives to the bees, simply because he does not like it, but does like them (**102**). Beneath his sometimes gruff exterior lies great sensitivity and thought for others; sometimes these are recognised, as in his relationships with the old *curé* and with Edmond, but more often they are not, as with the unmerited telling-off he gets from his aunt during his leave (**64**).

Firmin, in fact, treats others far better than they treat him. This concern for others, together with his moral integrity, his generosity and his lack of materialism, are qualities he shares with his priest cousin Edmond. Indeed, seen in conjunction with the nature and simplicity of Firmin's way of life, they bring to mind the existence of a monk, or rather a hermit, since he lives alone rather in a community; one might think that conscious prayer is the only element missing in this context. Firmin, however, is not very good at praying—when he spends the night watching beside the body of his friend the old *curé,* he does not even know 'comment ni à qui adresser un essai de prière' (**97**). Perhaps he does not need to. When Edmond Michelet was in Dachau, he had a communist friend who took his place each day at Mass at a time when he was too ill to go himself. This involved taking a considerable personal risk, as it did for Edmond Michelet himself (*21,* p. 205). For Firmin too, 'il lui suffisait d'offrir sa présence et son amitié' (**97**). If to love one's neighbour is to love God, what prayer could be better? This is not to portray Firmin as a conscious Christian (see Chapter Four), but he behaves better than many in the book who are, or who profess to be.

Edmond

For the child Firmin, Edmond had been 'un garçon doux et un peu bébête' (**13-14**), more inclined to dutiful obedience than to revolt—in this last respect the wartime episode of the crow's nest shows that neither of the cousins, in a sense, had changed. But maturity had led Firmin to arrive at a proper respect for his cousin's qualities. There is, for instance, no malice in the way he addresses him as 'curé', and probably concern as well as curiosity when he wonders how Edmond had put up with the bullying atmosphere of national service (**14**). In France, seminarists were not exempted from military service as they were in England and could be called up in wartime even when they became priests. Although Firmin's cousin has not yet been ordained, he is at an advanced state of training for the priesthood and clearly has clerical status. Members of the clergy were not obliged to fight when called up; they could undertake non-combatant duties instead.

Edmond, after starting the war as a stretcher-bearer, asks to be put in Firmin's fighting regiment. This is a very significant gesture, since it denotes his acceptance, despite his detestation of war (**49**), of the responsibility of all Frenchmen, including the clergy, actively to defend the Republic against unjust aggression. Not all of the clergy at the time acted as Edmond does; most of them, understandably, held that it was wrong for a priest to kill—even an unjust aggressor. Some may also have felt revulsion at fighting for a Republic which, they felt, had so recently been persecuting them. Edmond's gesture can thus be seen as having a symbolic value in the healing process that was gradually to bring closer the two previously antagonistic factions. It should also be noted that priests who refused to fight were no less brave and patriotic than the rest; very many of them distinguished themselves and gained the respect of all as stretcher-bearers, treating the wounded and bringing them back, often under fire, and many were killed or wounded.

Edmond and Firmin become, in the trenches, 'un tandem cocasse, tout pétri de contradictions, mais qu'une amitié solide, quoique bourrue, liait chaque jour davantage' (**55**), and this friendship endures to the end. As we have seen, they share the same personal qualities: courage, honesty, generosity, unselfishness, concern for others, lack of materialism. In fact they hold most values in common and their lifetyles are, to a great extent, remarkably similar. As Firmin gives away the fruits from his garden, Edmond spends his few savings on a radio set in order to reintegrate his cousin into society by getting him interested in what is happening in the world outside (**120**). Both men lead lives of what might be called evangelical poverty, the antithesis of that love of money which is said to be the root of all evil. In Edmond's case, however, the poverty is literally evangelical, since his whole life, and his values, are consciously based on the Gospel he has adhered to by becoming a priest. Moreover, becoming a priest in itself required courage at that time in 'un bourg farouchement républicain' such as Les Landes (**7**).

Like Firmin, Edmond is intellectually honest and free from the hypocrisy that characterises others in the village; he is willing to act according to his conscience and accept the consequences rather than to follow either popular fashion or his personal interests. Where Edmond differs from Firmin is in his quieter, more serious nature, brought out and emphasised by the weight of his responsibilities as a priest. In this latter capacity he is not bigoted, morover, any more than his predecessor as *curé* had been, and this at a time when clerical and anticlerical pressures were polarising society and pushing people on both sides towards bigotry. Edmond is not prim, either. Although he frequently reproves Firmin for swearing, what he objects to are not Firmin's crudities (e.g. the names he calls his donkey—**103**) but his oaths, because for him they are hurtful and blasphemous, since they belittle the God he loves and to whom he has dedicated his life.

Edmond's whole life is devoted to loving and serving the God to whom he has consecrated himself by becoming a priest. He does this by carrying out the duties that this entails, by constant, but usually discreet, prayer, as when setting out for the war (**51**) and by serving his fellow human beings. This conscious dedication of his life and service to God marks a key difference between him and Firmin. When appointed as parish priest, Edmond, like his predecessor, devotes himself to all the inhabitants of the village, whether they go to church or not. Both men are concerned less with proselytising than with bringing the love of God to where it is needed. Thus when Edmond persuades, or rather, virtually blackmails, Firmin into becoming sacristan, even though his religious beliefs are, to say the least, vague, it is because it will restore his human dignity and bring him back from total isolation and into village society again.

Edmond's friendship with Firmin is not, however, just a one-way affair. Each in turn takes care of the other. When Firmin is living in isolation, it is Edmond who looks after him, but in the trenches it is Firmin who takes the same role of protective elder brother to

Edmond, although he is quite capable of leading him into scrapes like the crow's nest affair (**55-61**). He is particularly supportive towards his cousin when the latter tells him of Émile's death on Firmin's return from leave in Les Landes. Firmin's news of Berthe is immediately overshadowed by Edmond's grim announcement. Firmin, untypically, makes a philosophical observation: if Edmond's God is good, then he is behaving strangely in allowing such things to happen. Edmond reacts passionately, putting the blame not on God but firmly on the human race for misusing its freedom to choose between good and evil, and he does so in soldier's vernacular, echoing Firmin's own choice of language. Firmin immediately notices Edmond's tears of anger, fatigue and grief and with his usual tact and strong practical sense offers him his grog bottle and some good advice: 'Pour le moment, faut pas trop penser à ça, faut juste penser à sauver sa carcasse...' (**66**).

Despite their differing characters, then, the two cousins support and complement each other. Thanks to Edmond's return to the village, Firmin regains his self-confidence and his sense of humour, but he in turn is able somehow to repay Edmond by making him smile, as by his zany comments on the old sacristan's beard (**104**). Many years later, during the Occupation, he also keeps a discreet eye on his cousin's Resistance activities, although, as already mentioned, Edmond will not let him be actively involved because Firmin's sympathies are too well known (**128-30**). Edmond clearly shares Firmin's views on the village mayor and his fellow self-seeking collaborators, but the need to keep a low profile, and, no doubt, Christian charity, prevent him from expressing them as truculently.

Given Edmond's first name and his saintly, unselfish personality, one might guess, as I have done (*24*), that his character may have been based to some degree on that of the writer's father. If so, the influence was an unconscious one, for the name was in fact chosen as being a typical one of the period, and the character of Edmond had been seen originally as a minor one. He had in fact been put in as a mere foil to Firmin, but as the latter became more and more cut off and silent, it became clear that someone would be needed to make him talk, or he would really go mad. Edmond's return to the village as parish priest solved the problem. It also meant that his role grew in importance from then on until he became the major character that he is (*Int*). In Claude Michelet's *La Grande Muraille,* as has happened for many another writer, a character took on a life of its own and changed the course of the plot.

Chapter Four

La Grande Muraille: significance

The question of what lies behind *La Grande Muraille* was the subject
of an article which I wrote about the book (*24*). The idea of the wall
in the title cannot but strike the reader as symbolic. What, though,
does this particular wall stand for, in both the literal and
metaphorical senses of that verb? Like the Great Wall of China, of
which we are inevitably reminded, and like other walls, its obvious
prime function is to serve as a boundary and keep out intruders.
Firmin, back from the war, makes the point when he first comes to
the realisation of what he is going to do with his stony field: 'ma
muraille fermera ma pièce' (**76**). It does more than that, however,
since Firmin soon becomes a virtual prisoner of his wall. It is true,
of course, that some time passes before anything like a wall is visible
above the surrounding stones, so that we need to distinguish the wall
itself from the task of constructing it. Yet almost as soon as he sets
about the task of clearing his field, and long before his wall is
recognisable, Firmin finds that he is figuratively on one side of it
and that the rest of the world is on the other.

It is not that he wants to exclude the outside world, for we have
seen that he is basically a merry, outgoing character, willing to help
his neighbours, popular with the girls and, as village barber, an asset
to the general social life of Les Landes. It is the refusal of his fellow
villagers to accept him on his own terms that leads them to exclude
him: 'ce furent les autres qui le poussèrent dans le silence, qui
échafaudèrent autour de lui un autre mur, un mur d'indifférence, et
de mépris amusé' (**92**). The process is inevitable, given their narrow-
mindedness and his stubbornness. Once he takes up the poisoned
chalice that his uncle's legacy represents, he has to drink its contents,
just as his uncle had intended, although it is doubtful whether his
uncle realised quite how far his petty malice would lead.

The inevitability with which Firmin's story develops and the
misery it brings for him bring to mind some of the ingredients of a
classical tragedy, though it clearly lacks many of the others. But to
pursue the tragic parallel for a moment, Firmin, in taking up his
uncle's gauntlet, does display the kind of overweening pride which

we usually associate with tragic heroes. The old *curé* puts his finger
on it in comparing Firmin's first acceptance of the challenge (**41**)
with the Old Testament story of the Tower of Babel, which the
people set about building in order to reach Heaven; the Almighty
reduced their arrogant plan to chaos by replacing their one common
language by a multitude of tongues (*Genesis,* XI: 1-9). But shortly
after he returns from the war, Firmin assures Edmond that he,
unlike the villagers, has given up any idea of a challenge (**86**). We
have already examined the rather desperate conversation he has with
himself some time later, denouncing the villagers' cowardice and
grandly declaring that his wall will be built 'et restera debout
pendant des siècles...' One might think at this point that the
overweening pride had returned were it not for the fact that he is
deeply depressed at the time and attempting to raise his own low
morale. The attempt, moreover, is to a great extent successful and
the judgments that he is then able to make on himself and the
villagers are more balanced, as can be seen in the conclusion he
comes to almost in the next sentence: 'je fais ce que je dois faire et
j'y trouve ma vie, ça me suffit' (**94**). This is a far saner view of both
his task and his life than had been his earlier, temporary reaction
and, later, Edmond's return to the village makes that life much less
unhappy.

Perhaps a better parallel for the *démesure* implied by Firmin's
defiant taking up of his uncle's challenge and the gigantic task he
undertakes in building the wall could be found in the epic. Once
again one must not exaggerate it, but Firmin's willingness to stand
apart from the herd and take on an impossible task at whatever cost
does contain a trace of epic grandeur. One thinks, momentarily, of
Milton's Satan, 'Who durst defy th'Omnipotent to arms' but clearly
such a comparison cannot be sustained. A better one can perhaps be
made with the 'village Hampden' of Gray's famous *Ode.*

There is such a thing as a local epic. One example of it (which,
however, certainly had no influence on *La Grande Muraille*) is to be
found in Frédéric Mistral's Provençal poem *Mirèio* (Mireille),
published in 1859. *Mirèio* is set in the contemporary rural society of
the lower Rhône valley and tells the story of a rich farmer's
daughter who falls in love with a poor basket-weaver's son. Mistral's
observance of the conventions of the Virgilian epic serves to give
greater stature to his characters, but their own clear-cut simplicity
already gives them a certain grandeur at their own level. Firmin, in
his own way, shows similar qualities. Clearer evidence of this kind

of epic dimension is to be found in Claude Michelet's later works, notably in *Des grives aux loups,* with its portrait of the obstinate patriarch Jean-Edouard, whose three children rebel against him and leave home one by one.

Despite his physical courage, proved, if proof were needed, by the decorations for bravery he wins in the First World War and the way he stands up both to collaborators and to the ill-disciplined *maquisards* in the Second, Firmin is vulnerable. Whilst his wall cuts him off from the villagers (and one must not forget that they could quickly remove his unhappiness by accepting him), it does at the same time provide him with a means for sheltering his vulnerability. The wall is therefore both a prison and a refuge. In theory, Firmin could escape from his prison by giving up his project, but, given the double bind that Edmond identifies (**86**), doing that would bring him as much mockery as would persisting with his plans, so the wall's function as a refuge is an essential one for him. Yet by persisting with his project he is at least able him to assert and preserve the independence which is so dear to him. So although Firmin is trapped behind his wall, the wall also constitutes the outward and visible sign of his independence.

The challenge and its consequences

Firmin's project is immediately seen by all in the village as the taking up of his uncle's challenge (although we have seen that after the war he drops all idea of a contest). As the years go by and the wall grows in size and beauty, Firmin's achievement makes him the clear winner of any contest there may have been between the two men; indeed, Firmin makes the very valid point that his uncle had already lost it at the start by dying (**76-7**). In the end, however, he gets no credit for his achievement, for by the time the wall and its garden have become a reality, the villagers, too, have forgotten all idea of a contest, and still see Firmin as a madman. This is not, moreover, the only price he has to pay for living in the shadow of his wall. He is also prevented from living a normal life and his greatest regret, as he muses on his deathbed, is that he has never had children to confer on his life use and meaning (**157**).

Yet Firmin's decision to build the wall, whose construction takes up the whole of his lifetime after he returns from the war, is not taken lightly. He decides what to do with his field through an

apparent revelation, a call—'sa véritable vocation'—which is in fact
the outcome of a long process of unconscious thought (76). There
are some clues as to what brings the decision about and to why the
wall, for Firmin, becomes more important than the field itself. When
he visits the field in the evening of the day when he becomes its
owner, his first thought is to clear and cultivate it, but he then
realises that in order to get all the stones out of the way he would
need to build a wall two metres high (23). What strikes him from
the very start, however, is the beauty of the place (20)—not,
incidentally, the reaction of a typical local rustic—, and it is this
aesthetic aspect which from then onwards dominates his thinking
about his project. One of his first ideas is to dig holes and plant trees
in them, but he realises that this is unrealistic and that the idea of
having to bend down to pick the fruit from the holes would be
grotesque. He therefore decides to make a start by clearing away the
heaps of stones so as to make the place look less nightmarish: 'Il opta
pour l'esthétique de l'entreprise' (30). He continues with the
clearance work until he goes to the war and he returns to it during
his first leave. His second leave is spent in Paris, and of all the
buildings there, the one that makes the greatest impression on him is
Notre-Dame. This is not, as it would have been for most people,
because of the thought of the enormous number of workers that must
have been needed to erect such a massive structure, but because one
individual, on a particular day, had had the idea of building it (68).

Firmin the artist

When he gets back from the war, Firmin, as we have seen,
suddenly realises what he wants to do—or, perhaps, rather, what he
must do: 'faire une muraille [...] avec des pierres que je rangerai et
chacune aura la place qu'elle devra avoir...' (76). What this tells us is
that Firmin is an artist at heart, and that his wall, 'l'œuvre de sa vie'
(92) is above all else a thing of beauty; the alcoves he builds in his
wall, especially the second, roofed by a perfect cupola-shaped vault
(121), are splendidly executed. His garden and orchard, too, are
things of great beauty, even though he may be the only person who
appreciates that beauty. Some of the garden's features, indeed, are
known only to himself, such as the private sundial which he makes
by planting a tall poplar tree so that its shadow will fall in turn on
the twelve apple trees that surround it (89).

As well as being an expert garden designer, Firmin is also a self-taught architect or, at least, civil engineer, and his competence is proved by the fact that his wall obeys the first principle of those professions: it stays upright, and clearly will do so for many a long year. But his work does not gain the recognition of others, since it is not constructed according to any other aesthetic principles than his own. Certainly the villagers see no value whatsoever in the idea of anyone's building any kind of wall on that scale and to no apparent purpose. One might say that lack of recognition should not matter to Firmin, since his aim had been the 'creation d'un univers dont il se réservait l'entière jouissance' (**77**). Yet others dismiss his work because they think it useless—even Edmond openly says so on one occasion, although at the time he is upset and concerned for Firmin (**115**)—and their lack of comprehension clearly must hurt him.

Every artist needs a public of some kind. Yet Firmin even has difficulty in persuading Edmond that his wall, which by then his cousin at least seems to recognise as being beautiful, does not have to serve any other purpose than to be beautiful, like any other work of art (**115-16**). Firmin all but quotes the words of Jesus, doubtless remembered from one of the old *curé*'s catechism classes during his childhood, telling the disciples that if they seek God and do what is right, God will supply all their needs: 'Why worry about clothing? Think of the lilies growing in the fields; they never have to work or spin; yet [...] Solomon in all his regalia was never robed like one of these' (*Matthew*, VI: 28-9). Flowers and butterflies, says Firmin, serve only to be beautiful, and his wall serves the same purpose. Edmond immediately understands; indeed he preaches his next sermon on the subject of flowers, whose beauty is given by God for the enjoyment of human beings. His congregation, however, understand the words only in their most superficial sense and apply them not to Firmin, as Edmond intended, but to their own selfish preoccupations.

Firmin's attitude to life and art may remind the English reader of W.H. Davies's famous lines: 'What is this life if, full of care, / We have no time to stand and stare?', but standing and staring is not Firmin's style. He is no slacker; in fact he probably works harder than his neighbours—he has to in order to complete his wall in the time left to him—and he works very efficiently. He begs no favours of others; the only request he makes to his fellow villagers is for cowpats, and he repays them for these with fruit from his garden, besides keeping the village clean (**89-91**). They reject and ridicule his work because it does not have an immediate use, but neither does that of most artists. Professional artists set out to make a living by selling their work to appreciative clients and some succeed in doing so; other artists may not wish to or need to. Sometimes, works which do not immediately command a market may fetch millions of pounds after the artist has died in poverty. In that sense Firmin's lack of recognition is not an infrequent fate, but at least he is in no danger of starving and he has only himself to please.

On one level, then, *La Grande Muraille* might be seen as drawing our attention to the fact that even a humble, ordinary person like Firmin is capable of producing something that can be seen, if only in his own eyes, as a work of art. (There is, perhaps another parallel to be made with the artist's life: when *La Grande Muraille* was published, some of the more pretentious Parisian critics must have wondered whether an author who happened to be a small farmer in the Corrèze was capable of producing a worthwhile novel...). Indeed Firmin, like his creator, is easy to underestimate. The argument we have just seen him using to Edmond, namely that his wall exists in order to be beautiful, is that of Art for Art's sake in its purest form; moreover he proves his artistic integrity after the initial phase when he drops all idea of a challenge and sets about building his wall simply for its own sake, without any other motive. Firmin's espousal of *l'art pour l'art* is not, of course, a philosophical pose; it is purely instinctive. It can be applied to him since it describes his own position; he certainly does not put it forward as a theory of aesthetics; as we know, he is far from being an intellectual.

Firmin's 'folly'

The artistic tradition that Firmin belongs rather to is a rather different one. Its exponents were at one time confined to members of the wealthier classes, often aristocrats, but their ranks have increased in more recent years as leisure and resources have become more widely available. In earlier times, rich eccentrics built—or, rather, hired others to build—'follies'. These were usually towers or similar monuments which served no practical purpose. They were often sited on hilltops, where they rapidly became local landmarks, and some of them are very handsome. In more recent times, humbler souls, often retired people, have taken up the tradition on a smaller scale, with varying degrees of aesthetic taste, sometimes decorating their gardens with curious objects or collections of exotic seashells. At its lowest level, the tradition manifests itself in the bevies of plastic gnomes that people many a suburban garden. Some of the more spectacular gardens, often at the seaside, can become very popular and make impressive sums for local charities. The tradition is probably more widely known in Britain, but there have been spectacular examples of it in France. One such, mentioned by Claude Michelet (*Int*), is that of one Chevalier, the postman at Hauterives (Drôme), whose Palais Idéal, built from stones picked up on his rounds between 1879 and 1912, is a major local tourist attraction there. Another, but much less well known, example is, of course, that of M. Faurel and his wife, the builders of the wall at Chartrier that inspired our novel. Firmin, like them, belongs with the greatest exponents of the tradition, all the more so since he builds his wall with his own hands and devotes the whole of his life to the task.

Unfortunately, as we have seen, Firmin is not accorded the understanding and tolerance that are given to eccentrics in our own day (and that were given to rich ones in former times). Indeed nowadays such people may not even be considered as eccentric, whereas the harsh intolerance and ridicule that Firmin meets with when he embarks on his project are stoked up in advance by the mockery which his uncle's legacy provokes. The difference in attitudes over time is perhaps an indication that some little progress has been made in Britain and France as regards this particular aspect of social life, although examples of intolerance and its awful consequences in other fields, political, racial and religious, daily fill the news media.

The small farmer's struggle

In seeking to interpret the symbolism of *La Grande Muraille*, we should not forget the problems which the author had to face at the time when he was writing it. We have already touched on some of them in the context of *La Grande Muraille*. They are further illustrated, as we shall see, in his later novel *Rocheflame*. Placed in this context, *La Grande Muraille* can be seen at one level to symbolise the life and problems of the French small farmer, whose way of life, in the view of certain economists, seems to be as pointless as Firmin's. The large-scale practitioners of agribusiness have vast hedgeless fields and huge, expensive machinery, but in areas like the Corrèze, the fields are too small to take such machines, even if the farmers could afford them. They cannot make more than a basic living from their land, so they are dismissed as being inefficient. Yet as Claude Michelet makes clear, both in *Rocheflame* and the polemical *Cette terre est la vôtre* (*7*; *8*), the small farmer still has an important role to play and his recompense for all his hard work and worry is that he keeps his independence and that the land is beautiful; like Firmin wondering what to do with his stony field, the hero of *Rocheflame* decides to 'opt[er] pour l'esthétique' (**30**). Many small farmers in France and elsewhere must, however, ask themselves at times, as Firmin does at the end, what is the point of their existence. At least the hero of *Rocheflame,* Michel, like his creator, sees his life as being worth while and embarks on the future with hope and realism, if not with confidence.

In the broader, but allied, context of developments which have taken place in the economic and political fields since the book first appeared in 1969, *La Grande Muraille* can be seen as sounding a prophetic note against the prevailing cult of utilitarianism, in the sense of a doctrine which judges everything by the profits it makes in the short term and where the 'bottom line' is the sole measure of everything. In practice the so-called efficiency which is pursued can lead to real inefficiency in the long term, while at the same time harming both the environment and human beings. The theme was one which the author was to treat in more detail in his subsequent writings about E.C. agricultural policies, such as that of reducing surpluses by radically reducing the number of small farmers. Another such policy is 'set aside': so as not to grow unsaleable produce, farmers are paid not to cultivate some of their land, which may then become overgrown with scrub and weeds, both likely to catch fire in hot weather. Since, because of both mechanisation and E.C. policies, there are fewer and fewer farmers left in the countryside to fight them, such fires are liable to reach disastrous proportions, so the apparent saving is not a real one. The principle is also applicable in many other contexts.

If we view it in this light as an attack on utilitarianism, *La Grande Muraille* might be seen, like *Rocheflame,* as a contribution to 'green' literature (see M. Parry's article, *26*). It is also intriguing to note in this context that the apparently useless wall which M. Faurel and his wife built at Chartrier eventually inspired a novel which has given pleasure to many thousands of readers and that the wall continues to impress the visitors who go to view both it and the village.

Firmin, philosopher or believer?

In my article on *La Grande Muraille* I noted the resemblance between Firmin and the mythological character Sisyphus, chosen by Camus to be the hero of *Le Mythe de Sisyphe*. Both characters spend their lives handling large stones. For Camus, the fate of Sisyphus, forever condemned to roll a particularly large stone up to the top of a hill, only to see it inevitably roll down again, represents what he calls the absurdity of the human condition, against which we should all revolt. Firmin loses his father in an absurd accident and his mother soon after, has a not very happy childhood, is then thrown into the absurd slaughter of the trenches and goes on to spend the rest of his life moving stones in order to construct an absurdly useless wall; the total irrelevance of the wall at Chartrier to any practical purpose was what most impressed Michelet about it when he came to write his book (*Int*). Firmin might therefore seem to be a perfect example of a Camusian *homme révolté,* particularly since his childhood and youth are one long revolt against his uncle and aunt.

Another literary parallel (though, as with Camus, without the suggestion of an influence) could be made between Firmin's behaviour and that of the hero at the end of Voltaire's *Candide*. In it Voltaire, the apostle of anticlericalism, but probably unknown except perhaps by name to the anticlerical Firmin, explores the human condition and the problem of evil. After undergoing all kinds of adventures and misadventures, and considering all the conflicting philosophical theories put forward to explain them, Candide comes to the conclusion that, rather than bother with theories, 'il faut cultiver son jardin'. Firmin goes one better; he turns a barren waste into a garden as well as building his wall (to which the garden, admittedly, is secondary) and he displays a similar attitude of practical common sense to the one which Candide finally displays when he is faced with the horrors of life—the offer of his *gnôle* to the despairing Edmond is a typical example (**66**).

In that sense, Firmin has perhaps more in common with Voltaire than with Camus (apart from the anachronism involved in connecting him with the latter). Yet it would be wrong too closely to connect him with either, for his approach to life is one which is instinctively and immediately practical, not one which first examines and then rejects philosophical theories. As his author says, Firmin 'ne plonge pas dans des abîmes de métaphysique' (*Int*). The need he feels to rebel against his uncle, and thus against the injustice of fate, is above all a physical need (**13**), because he is very much a physical person; that is how he expresses himself.

Yet he is neither stupid nor insensitive and he has a good sense of humour, as we have seen. It is true that he finds it hard to express both abstract ideas and deep feelings, although he manages to express the latter perfectly well in his own way, both to himself (**94**) and to Edmond when discussing his isolation (**100**) and he even manages, also in his own way, to convey his 'philosophy of art' to his cousin: the purpose of his wall is to be beautiful, and that is enough for him (**115-16**). However, the old *curé*'s references to the Tower of Babel (**41**) and Edmond's to an ideal (**49**) leave him puzzled, and when he learns from Edmond about his brother Émile's death, he finds himself in really deep water as he tries to fathom the mystery of the problem of evil. It is, as we have just noted, by means of a physical gesture—the offer of his grog bottle—that he manages to express his love and sympathy for his cousin. This gesture, incidentally, is a good illustration of one of the major achievements of the book, which is the author's successful portrayal, in Firmin, of the hidden depths to be found in 'ordinary' people who are capable of extraordinary deeds and who have strong sensitivities and deep feelings, even though they may not be very intellectual and are, perhaps, not very articulate when it comes to expressing those feelings.

The ending of *La Grande Muraille,* with Firmin's receiving the Last Sacraments at his own request and asking Edmond to bless his wall, raises the question of Firmin's religious beliefs. One should note here the resemblance between Firmin's end and that of Pierre-Édouard, the central character of the Saint-Libéral trilogy. When he realises that he is nearing death, at the end of the last volume, *L'Appel des engoulevents,* the eighty-eight-year-old Pierre-Édouard sends for the *curé,* even though he has never been noted for churchgoing during his lifetime. He makes this gesture because he knows it will please his wife; it is, in fact, a final act of love for her. Firmin's action, too, is done to please his friend and cousin Edmond and is a similar valedictory demonstration of devotion. Both acts are completely in accord with the Christian spirit of love for one's neighbour. But does that make Firmin a Christian, and if so, to what extent?

We have already noted that in practice Firmin, like Edmond, leads
a life of almost evangelical simplicity, that he is upright in morals
(apart from his occasional excursions *en ville*), is dedicated to his
chosen task and is devoted to his two priest friends, in spite of their
political differences. Furthermore, he is detached from wealth and
generously gives away the produce of his garden to others. He may
have arguments with others but we never hear him calumniate them
and the words he uses to the old *curé* at the end of the war could well
be those of a Trappist monk: 'Le monde, il ne m'intéresse pas,
surtout depuis la guerre...' (**79**). So the contrast between Firmin and
most of his fellow villagers—grasping, materialistic, backbiting,
always seeing the worst in others, yet supposed, many of them, to be
Christians—is all to his advantage and in this, as we have seen, he
resembles his cousin Edmond.

Where Edmond differs radically from Firmin is in his strong
religious faith, a faith which is so strong that he devotes his whole
life to it by becoming a priest. It is clear, however, that before he
becomes sacristan, Firmin has not darkened the door of a church
since his childhood (when he was, no doubt, made to go). Certainly
his knowledge of religious doctrine seems sketchy; although the story
of the Tower of Babel (**41**) is far from central to Christianity, his
ignorance of it is probably symptomatic. Moreover, he is a professed
anticlerical, an attitude which is in keeping with his own adversarial
temperament as well as the general political outlook of the village.
He expresses his anticlericalism strongly, although in a good-
humoured way, through jokes directed at the old *curé* and Edmond,
both of whom take them in the spirit in which they are meant.
Anticlericalism, of course, is not incompatible with religion—indeed
some of the Catholic Church's firmest adherents over the centuries
have fiercely criticised the clergy of their day.

Yet Firmin's views overall do not lead one to think of him as
being even a lukewarm believing Christian. When Edmond asks him
to become sacristan, he has to do a great deal of persuading; Firmin
thinks himself to be quite unsuitable and also unworthy. This
reaction is typical of him and shows clearly his respect for genuine
religion. He protests his lack of faith: 'j'y crois pas beaucoup', yet his
anticlericalism has not made him anti-religious: 'je suis pas contre'
(**105**); clearly, if he had been, Edmond would not have asked him to
be sacristan. The answer to his last question to Edmond, 'T'as
vraiment besoin de moi?' (**106**), shows, above all, Firmin's pleasure
at this mark of confidence as well as his willingness to help his

cousin. Then, when he does take up his duties, he carries them out in an exemplary way, just as he would with any other task; yet he does slip out to do haircuts during Sunday sermons, having carefully timed several of the latter so as to judge their average length (**109**).

When Firmin is taken ill and realises that his end is near, he asks Edmond to hear his confession and to administer what was then called Extreme Unction, the last symbolic anointing with oil to strengthen the soul for its journey to the next life (it is nowadays known as the Sacrament of the Sick and not reserved only for the dying). His words are significant: 'tu veux que je finisse bien' (**156**). We have seen that he makes this request in order to please Edmond; he may also think it right and proper at the end of his life to ask pardon for past misdeeds; it is the normal thing to do. The final request he makes to Edmond, to bless his wall, is an important one; for Firmin, it will be a sign, a proof, that his life's work has not been in vain. In my article (*24*), I argued that without seeing Firmin as an active Christian, this gesture could be seen as a dedication of his work to God and the consequent transformation of his uncle's mean and negative gesture into a positive one. It is certain that by constructing his wall and its beautiful garden Firmin turns something mean into something fine, but the article seems to me now to make Firmin's end sound like a deathbed conversion.

Certainly Claude Michelet sees his request for a blessing more as the official confirmation, by 'une autorité', that he had not wasted his life and that it had been of some use (*Int*). Moreover Firmin does not need a death-bed conversion, for he dies as he has lived, close in many ways to the Christian ideal. He cannot be described as a believer yet in dying, as in living, he does what seems to him to be right and proper, and he dies with a clear conscience. From the point of view of Catholic theology, that is all that anyone needs to do. It is true that Firmin's religious beliefs remain vague to the end, but one does not have to be an expert theologian to be saved. The two statements quoted earlier, 'j'y crois pas beaucoup' and 'je suis pas contre', sum his beliefs up well and are very much in tune with the rest of his character. Firmin may be out of his depth in matters metaphysical, but his heart is in the right place. He tries to do good and avoid evil and, in his own way, to love his neighbour. In this respect he is like a good many other ordinary human beings. As has been noted, Claude Michelet's success in portraying so well and convincingly the ordinariness of Firmin is one of the outstanding features of *La Grande Muraille*.

Firmin, Edmond and Gaullist idealism

Firmin's relationship with Edmond, who started as a foil to
Firmin but became a major character, is an important feature of the
book. From mutual indifference in childhood and, later, opposing
ideologies, they grow to being inseparable during the war. Indeed,
after Edmond was wounded, the war, of course, continued, but
'Firmin la vécut seul, malgré ses camarades, car son cousin était
absent.' (72) Their friendship is renewed when Edmond returns to
the village as *curé*. The warmth of their relationship clearly
symbolises the gradual decline of the traditional bitterness between
clericals and anticlericals in France. It also echoes the experience of
Edmond Michelet and the friendships he found, both in the *Équipes
sociales* and later, in dire circumstances, when he was arrested and
sent to Dachau. It certainly celebrates the triumph of decency and
humanity over bigotry of all kinds. Given his father's Gaullist ideals,
which Claude shares, the story of Firmin and Edmond can perhaps
also be seen as reflecting the spirit of those ideals. This is clearly not
to be seen in any political party sense: the problem for Gaullists is
how to avoid becoming just another of the political parties whose
self-interest the General denounced. It is, rather, the spirit which
encouraged wartime Frenchmen to rise above their political and
ideological differences in order to save their country. The theme of
mutual tolerance and respect exemplified in *La Grande Muraille* by
the relationship between Firmin and Edmond (and also the old *curé*)
occurs often in Claude Michelet's later works, so also do the
machinations—often petty—of French local politics.

What above all attracted the author to write *La Grande Muraille*
when he first saw the wall at Chartrier and thought of transposing it
into a novel, was, as has already been said, its complete uselessness
for any practical purpose (*Int*). This might make one think of
Firmin's action in building his wall as the kind of *acte gratuit,* the
motiveless act, usually criminal, which has in the past fascinated
writers such as Gide. But once again this would be a totally
inappropriate attribution of metaphysical motives to Firmin. Besides,
'uselessness' is not to be confused with any lack of purpose or
satisfaction on the part of the builder. Firmin's job satisfaction would
be the envy of many people nowadays who find themselves doing
jobs which are considered 'useful' because they are 'productive', but
which are deeply boring and unsatisfying for them. Firmin's attitude
to work is an echo of the upbringing of Claude's father Edmond. He

had been taught, and taught his own children, to believe in the importance of what Charles Péguy called *le devoir d'état*. Each person's occupation and station in life brings with it certain duties. The important thing is to carry out those duties well, whether one's position is high or low. Péguy's family was poor; his mother was a *rempailleuse de chaises*—she repaired the straw seats of chairs (the kind that figure in Van Gogh's paintings). Yet she carried out this humble task to the best of her ability. Firmin's occupation may be an unusual one, but he carries it out in the same way.

Perhaps, then, on the widest and most general level, the wall stands for the task—whether at work or in our private life—which each of us has to face in life. This view of *La Grande Muraille* was admirably and, indeed, rather poignantly illustrated in a letter sent to the author. It came from someone who was not normally thought of as a critic of fiction—unless one includes in the latter category the sayings of politicians. The writer was Charles de Gaulle, then President of France. Claude Michelet had sent him a copy of his novel when it came out early in 1969. At the time, the country was in the midst of the political turmoil that had followed the near revolution that took place in the previous year. A referendum, in effect a vote of confidence in the President and, for him, a judgment on his life's work, was due to take place on 28 April 1969. The most, therefore, that the young author expected in the circumstances was a formal acknowledgement from a secretary. Instead, he received the following reply in the General's own handwriting:

Mon cher Claude Michelet,

Dans votre livre *La Grande Muraille,* il y a
beaucoup de sentiments, de couleurs, de
souvenirs, bref il y a la vie.

Je vous en fais mon bien sincère compliment.

Nous avons tous à bâtir notre grande muraille.
Certes aucun de nous n'achèvera jamais la sienne.
Mais avoir toujours voulu le faire, y avoir toujours
travaillé comme votre Firmin, n'est-ce pas, pour
nous aussi, la seule chose qui vaille la peine?

Veuillez croire, mon cher Claude Michelet, à
mes très sympathiques et dévoués sentiments.

Charles de Gaulle

The General had read the book and it had clearly made a considerable impression on him. At a time when he faced the possibility—which was soon to become a reality, for he lost the referendum and resigned—of having his life's work rejected by the French people, the self-doubts of the dying Firmin must have had a particular meaning for him. Yet he could certainly identify also with Firmin's lifelong faithfulness to the task he had undertaken despite all obstacles. De Gaulle's use of the phrase 'pour nous aussi' is not, I believe, the kind of usurpation of the imperial 'we' that characterises lesser beings; it implies, rather, a genuine recognition that he shared the same values, notably that of the *devoir d'état,* as his correspondent. It obviously also expresses strong personal feelings.

Taking this idea a little further, the wall and its construction can be seen as a metaphor for, and a formulation of, what is perhaps the ultimate question for human beings: the problem of our very existence and its purpose—or lack of a purpose. Firmin sets out to build his wall and continues with its construction throughout the years without ever being finally sure of the reason why. When he starts clearing the field in 1914, the old *curé* asks him what use his work is. In reply, Firmin asks the *curé* the same question about his own work and concludes: 'Vous, vous faites ce qui vous plaît et ça vous paraît important, pour moi, c'est tout comme!' (**40**). However, he continues to question himself about his motives over the years.

The self-questioning culminates in his dying plea to Edmond to reassure him by blessing the wall; even with his last breath he admits that he still does not know why he built it (**158**). As we have seen, Firmin is no intellectual and advances no philosophical theories, but on a practical level—the one that counts in this context - he certainly does not lead the kind of unexamined life that the great philosopher Plato condemns as being unlivable for a human being. In his own way, and to the best of his ability, Firmin tries hard to discover what the purpose of his life is. More importantly, he tries to live it accordingly, and his moral standards are high and decent ones. Unfortunately, his eccentricity, although it hurts no one else, meets with a hostile reaction which blinds others to his many good qualities. Such honesty as Firmin's is rare; the intolerance which it meets with is not. There, perhaps, lies the ultimate lesson of his story.

Chapter Five

After *La Grande Muraille*

A year after *La Grande Muraille,* in 1970, Michelet published what its title page described as a novel, *Une fois sept.* It was in fact a fictionalized account of the author's childhood before agricultural college. Subsequent editions restored the characters' real names to this often amusing and at times compelling account of the family's life during and after the war. Sadly, Edmond Michelet, its central figure apart from the author, died that same year. Amongst other works, Edmond had written a magnificent account of his arrest and imprisonment in Dachau, *Rue de la Liberté* (the title recalls the ironic name the prisoners gave to its main thoroughfare, *Freiheitstrasse*). Pressure of work and illness had prevented him from writing his memoirs, so Claude's biography, *Mon père Edmond Michelet,* published in 1971, drew on notes that his father had left, as well as on his own first-hand memories. It is thus an important historical source in its own right as well as being very readable.

Rocheflame

In 1973, Claude produced his second 'real' novel, *Rocheflame.* It tells the story of Michel Delabat, who after national service had taken over the small family farm rather than return to a boring office job. After ten years, he realises that the farm will not support them and that his wife is becoming desperate. Moreover, he has literary ambitions which she finds it hard to understand.

The autobiographical significance of *Rocheflame* was noted in Chapter One. The name Michel(et), the discovery of a literary vocation, partly as a means of escape from the boredom of army life, his friendship with Pierre Panen, the burning of Claude's own early typescripts, the early struggles with his farm are all to be found in it. Pierre Panen (*25,* pp. 89-90) also notes the resemblances between Marcillac and the house in the novel.

The autobiographical parallels must not, however, be taken too far. *Rocheflame* shows the pressures placed on the marriages of small farmers, but one should not equate Claude's marriage with that of his fictional characters; his wife, unlike Françoise in the novel, was not reduced to taking a job in town to save the farm. *Rocheflame* describes the fictional couple's misunderstandings before they reach their decision. Françoise is puzzled by Michel's passion for writing, but she is even more puzzled when he burns his manuscript. It recounted the struggles of Jehan Bonavi, a fifteenth-century farmer, to save Rocsèche, their ancestral farmhouse, then called Rocheflame, from the clutches of his feudal lord. That story, like theirs, ends in hope: Jehan, although wounded, keeps his house and stays on the land. Other farming couples have not been as lucky, and one senses that the author's moral is 'There but for the grace of God go I'.

The medieval story in *Rocheflame* is well told. Fifteenth-century language, however, is very difficult for any writer to convey without its appearing quaint, although Michelet succeeds as well as most. The fictional author perhaps acknowledges the difficulty by burning his manuscript. Moreover, the inclusion of the rejected 'book within the book' is an unusual and potentially risky device. It says much for Claude Michelet's lack of smugness that he was prepared to take such a risk. Yet the plot of *Rocheflame* is ingenious, and the difficulties of life on a small farm are well conveyed. In particular, the efforts of the struggling writer Michel and his wife to overcome their misunderstandings and re-establish their relationship are sensitively and movingly portrayed.

All this certainly justifies *Rocheflame* as a novel. It also brings the problems of contemporary agriculture on to Claude Michelet's fictional scene for the first time (leaving aside the 'forgotten' *La Terre qui demeure*), though not for the last. The Saint-Libéral trilogy was later to examine the historical antecedents, the development and the effects of these same problems, in such a fascinating way as to gain the sympathy of the reader for the author's cause straight away, and without seeming to preach. In an article in *Francophonie* (26), Margaret Parry has analysed this aspect of *Rocheflame*, seeing it as a valuable contribution to 'green' literature by the author's use of the novel to make urban readers realise the importance of the small farmer. This theme, together with French agriculture in general, was to be given fuller treatment in Claude's next two books, neither of which was a novel.

The publisher Robert Laffont had written the volume 'Éditeur' for his firm's series 'Un homme et son métier'. Claude Michelet was introduced to its literary editor, Jacques Peuchmaurd, by a mutual friend, the novelist Michel Peyramaure, as being the best man to write about the life of a farmer. This was in 1973 at the first of the annual Book Fairs which are held in the magnificent Marché Georges Brassens in Brive (*25*, p. 91). Two years later, *J'ai choisi la terre* appeared under the Laffont imprint, as did most of Claude's subsequent works, including those published earlier by Julliard.

J'ai choisi la terre

J'ai choisi la terre continues Claude's autobiography after *Une fois sept,* recounting his schooling in Paris, his agricultural training, his national service and his life as a small farmer in the world of the Common Agricultural Policy. It also explains the reasons, many of them touched on in *Rocheflame*, why small farmers joined—and were joining—the *exode rural*: long working hours for them and their wives; houses without even basic comforts; expensive machinery, seeds and fertilisers; small returns stemming from low market prices; easier and better paid jobs available in town and irrational and inconsistent national and EC agricultural policies.

Claude tells us finally that despite all these problems (and at the time he was not well off) he stays on the land because he loves it, because it is beautiful; we again remember how Firmin, first faced with his chaotic stony field, 'opta pour l'esthétique' (**30**). Firmin's choice of 'le travail d'un homme libre' (**29**) also comes to mind in Claude's description of his job as giving him freedom and independence, despite having animals to feed and milk daily; he could cultivate his land and plan his time as he saw fit; success or failure were his responsibility alone (*7*, p. 204). Problems such as food surpluses, ecology and the proper use of pesticides and fertilisers are also discussed and the case for small hill farms is convincingly argued.

J'ai choisi la terre sold very well and was awarded the Prix des Volcans. It was followed, in 1977, by a second book on the subject of French agriculture. *Cette terre est la vôtre* examines French farming in general, and details the enormous changes that have taken place in the French countryside: life is difficult there nowadays and the very existence of villages and of rural life itself is threatened by the disappearance of institutions like the local school. These problems are very close to Michelet's heart, and throughout his literary career he has done a great deal to make them known through both books and journalism. They are at the heart of *Rocheflame,* and were to be equally prominent in the Saint-Libéral trilogy.

A new edition of his book, *Cette terre est toujours la vôtre,* came out in 1988, with extracts from his articles for *Agrisept / Le Nouvel Agriculteur* on more recent developments. The arguments the author advances are based on a long-term view of agriculture and its problems, and are informed by the same sense of history which is evident in his novels.

The Saint-Libéral Trilogy

The next book, *Des grives aux loups,* which appeared in 1979, is arguably the author's masterpiece and was to set him finally on the road to fame. It was the first volume of a trilogy about two families in a village in the Corrèze at the turn of the century. Like *La Grande Muraille,* it is an account of life in the fictitious locality of Saint-Libéral-sur-Diamond, one that is modelled on Madame Michelet's picturesque home village of Perpezac-le-Blanc, which nestles on a hillside about twenty kilometres to the west and north of Brive. The name Libéral is both that of a local saint, to whom a chapel is dedicated in Brive, and an expression of Claude Michelet's own personal convictions (*Int*).

The title of each volume of the trilogy refers to a bird; the author is an expert in ornithology and would have happily taken it up as a profession had he not become a farmer (*Int*). The opening of the first book explains its title. One winter afternoon late in 1899, two children, Pierre-Édouard and Louise Vialhe, are out in the snow with their friend Léon Dupeuch (the *ch* is pronounced 'k'). He has laid snares to catch thrushes, but they hear wolves howling and escape by leaving them the thrushes, to the great chagrin of Léon, who is loth to give up his prize—a possible omen of his future business success (see a reminiscence of this in *10,* pp. 195-6). His family are poor and when his sister Mathilde is born, in the first hour of 1900, Dr Fraysse (pronounced Fraïsse) leaves festive food and wine for her mother. This gift, and a bank account opened for the special new baby by the family's landlady, are seen as shaming charity by Léon's father, who hangs himself in despair, provoked in part by village gossips, like those who accuse Firmin of Alfred's death in *La Grande Muraille* (**8**). Léon, at thirteen, becomes the family breadwinner. The children remain friends. Pierre-Édouard leaves school to work on the farm for his highly authoritarian father, Jean-Édouard. One day he will take it over, but in the meantime he and his two sisters must obey. The book recounts their struggle to break free.

The ambitious Jean-Édouard joins the council, helps to bring the railway, and prosperity, to Saint-Libéral (and himself), and becomes mayor. His elder daughter Louise falls in love with a young railway surveyor, and he brutally sends her away to her cousins, having a richer husband in mind. She escapes and marries, but her parents disown her, and when her husband dies she goes into service to keep her young son rather than return home. Pierre-Édouard does his military service, but then stands his father's bullying for only a few days before seeking work elsewhere.

In 1914, he and Léon (now a successful cattle dealer) go to war. Berthe escapes to Paris and works as a nurse. Her brother, on leave, meets Léon's young sister, Mathilde. After the war they marry, but his parents refuse to recognise her, so they take a rented cottage. When Jean-Édouard's wife dies, however, his children—Louise, remarried but again a widow; Berthe, now running her own fashion house in Paris—rally round, and he tacitly accepts them and Mathilde. To spare the old man's pride, Pierre-Édouard lets him decide when he will hand over the family farm.

Des grives aux loups was an enormous success; it won the Prix des Libraires and its sales have exceeded two million. It clearly appeals to a deep instinct in its French readers, many of whom still have memories of, if not links with, country life: Pierre Panen points out (*25*, p. 105), that each identifies with a member of the Vialhe family and that they see their own relatives in the other characters.

The second volume of the trilogy, *Les Palombes ne passeront plus* (1980), continues the story from 1930, through the thirties' depression, World War Two and its aftermath, to 1968. The village steadily declines over the years, and when Pierre-Édouard celebrates his golden wedding to Mathilde he wonders if the migratory woodpigeons, the *palombes* of the title, will still visit Saint-Libéral in the future.

Since the events chronicled in *Les Palombes ne passeront plus* were so recent, the story of Saint-Libéral had to be put aside for a time. A trilogy centred on Chile, whose volumes succeeded each other from 1985 to 1988, came next, and the third volume of the Saint-Libéral series, *L'Appel des engoulevents*, not until 1990.

It is 1974. Léon is dead and Pierre-Édouard, much enfeebled, is living with his two sisters in Saint-Libéral. His son Jacques, now running the farm and mayor of the village, is struggling to keep both viable. The future looks bleak, but tourism and a *colonie de vacances* bring some hope, and the younger members of the Vialhe family, like nightjars (*engoulevents*), the birds of the title, still return to their home territory. The story ends as Pierre-Édouard, having learned of the birth of a great-grandson, dies a happy man.

The above brief summaries omit an enormous number of events and characters, major and minor, which together give a portrait of France as seen from the perspective of a village in the lower Corrèze during the first three quarters of the twentieth century. When it starts, transport, apart from trains, is horse-drawn, with cows often drawing ploughs and carts; it ends in the age of space travel. More striking are the changing mental and social attitudes. Before 1914, Jean-Édouard mocks superstitious villagers frightened by a *chasse volante*, the sound of migrating geese at night, which they believe are the souls of the dead. Yet he tyrannises his children, and wants to marry off his daughters against their wishes like a father in a Molière play. The liberated ladies of the 1970s are very different, having already been shown the way by Louise and Berthe.

Together with the sense of history which we see in this portrait of a changing society, there is also a sense of the continuing importance of the family and of the local community, with all their faults and virtues. (In this regard, if Firmin in *La Grande Muraille* is unlucky with his community, Edmond at least helps to redeem the honour of the family.) Behaviour in families may be reprehensible and through choice or necessity the young may leave, but in time of trouble they return. The village may be full of rivalries and vicious gossip (we remember the unjust treatment of Firmin and the suicide of Léon's father), but even in the busy 1970s neighbours rally round. The trilogy may thus be seen as making a contribution to the current debate on society and the family.

Of the three volumes, the first is undoubtedly the finest. It has simplicity on its side; life, if harder, was on the whole simpler in the early years of the century. Much that it portrays, both in farming methods and family relationships, had not changed for very many centuries: the authoritarian *paterfamilias* dates back to the Roman Empire. Seen in this light, the children's revolt against their father takes on the kind of epic tone already noted in *La Grande Muraille*.

The later volumes are also fine works: the characters are well drawn, and each develops with time. The community itself is a character in its own right, as in *La Grande Muraille*. The trilogy is a remarkable achievement.

The Chilean Trilogy

In 1981, under the strain of two full-time jobs and the many commitments that accompanied the success of *Les Palombes*, Claude Michelet's health understandably broke down. His wife took over the farm while he became perforce a full-time writer. As he had to look outside Saint-Libéral for the subject of his next book, he rotated the globe in his study and selected Chile (*Int*). He had visited Mexico and met the grandson of a Frenchman who had made his fortune there as a wandering trader, as did many inhabitants of the small town of Barcelonnette, in the Alpes de Haute-Provence. Indeed, Claude himself had a South American ancestor (*25*, pp. 137-8). The eventual result of all this—and of considerable subsequent researches—was a remarkable trilogy published over a period of just four years.

The first volume, *Les Promesses du ciel et de la terre* (1985), recounts the adventures of two young Frenchmen, Martial Castagnier, a travelling wine merchant from Lodève, and Antoine Leyrac, a farmer from the Corrèze, who become friends in 1871 in the turmoil following the Franco-Prussian War. Martial, who has rescued a young *repasseuse*, Pauline, from marauding soldiers while in Paris, is asked by a Bordeaux businessman to open a trading post in Chile. Antoine marries Pauline, Martial marries Rosemonde, his mistress from Bordeaux, and they all set sail. The men at first travel the country in a covered wagon, selling tools and cooking pots, while their wives open a fashion shop in the capital, Santiago, and together they build up prosperous businesses of their own while undergoing many hardships and adventures.

The second volume, *Pour un arpent de terre*, finds them involved in the war which Chile fought in 1879-1884 against its northern neighbours, Bolivia and Peru, over their frontier deserts (Voltaire, in Chapter 23 of *Candide*, had talked of France and England fighting over 'quelques arpents de neige' in Canada, but these deserts were rich in minerals). Antoine and Martial have many more adventures in this dangerous environment; they make more friends and their loyalty to Chile brings them further success.

The final volume of the trilogy, *Le Grand Sillon,* came out in 1988, a century after the unsuccessful French attempt, made by Ferdinand de Lesseps, the builder of the Suez Canal, to join the Atlantic and Pacific Oceans via the Panama isthmus. The conditions were appalling: there were hills covered in tropical rain forest for the canal to cross and disease was rife. Antoine and Martial operate dredging equipment for the project and stay on until it fails in 1889, creating a great financial scandal. Martial returns to France and Antoine will follow when their children grow up.

Like the Saint-Libéral trilogy, the Chilean novels, of which the above gives the barest of summaries, are firmly based on history. They depict the capital and rural France just after the 1870 War, Paris during the 1878 Exhibition, the many and varied landscapes of Chile and the construction of the Panama Canal, detailing the working conditions, the civil engineering involved, and the wildlife of the surrounding jungles. Yet the detail is not gratuitous, or the exoticism self-indulgent; they convey authenticity and show the enormous contrast between the world the characters have left and the one in which they make their new life. That world can be savage— the descriptions of the wartime assault on the fort at Arica and of the sack of Lima are terrifying—and is seen through the eyes and values of the characters. We are left to draw our own conclusions, for instance, when a rich woman declares that the common people are fit only for flogging, or when we read of the appalling injuries inflicted on local *peones* by unfamiliar machinery or dynamite.

The trilogy is more than an adventure story, however. The historical background illustrates the local effects of the rivalries between European powers over access to markets during this period of colonial expansion, and the descriptions of the activities of trading companies and bankers ring true. Equally authentic, no doubt, is the portrayal of the lives of luxury led by some; at about this time the Brazilian town of Manaos, a thousand miles up the Amazon, had its own opera house, visited by singers from Europe. The conspicuous consumption of luxury goods by the rich in the face of desperate poverty is, moreover, still a feature of life both in South America and elsewhere. The three books convey both the spirit of adventure (often inspired by economic desperation) which impelled many Europeans to seek a better life overseas during the nineteenth century, and the power of friendship, an indispensable means of survival in any pioneer society.

La Nuit de Calama

La Nuit de Calama (1994), Claude Michelet's latest novel, cleverly brings together the two trilogies. In *L'Appel des engoulevents,* the photographer Christian Leyrac, whose *Corrézien* great-grandfather had lived in Chile, married Jacques Vialhe's niece, Josyane. In 1979, reporting in Chile under the Pinochet dictatorship, he is arrested and detained for a night in the small town of Calama. The sound of a woman prisoner sobbing in despair during the night reminds him of his search for his own father, of whom his mother had said only that he had died through being in the Resistance.

Having found the former Leyrac house in the Corrèze, Christian, advised by Jo's aunt Berthe, a Ravensbrück survivor, writes to former *résistants* and thus learns the truth from Jean Salviac, of the Château Armandine vineyard in the Médoc. He is the son of Martial and Rosemonde Castagnier's daughter Armandine, whose name the vineyard bears, and of Félicien Salviac, a wine merchant. Jean was born in 1915, as was Christian's father, Adrien, the grandson of Martial's companions Antoine and Pauline Leyrac. Their son Marcelin had studied in France, returning there later from Chile to marry a Frenchwoman. When she died, their son Adrien was brought up with Jean on the Salviac estate and they remained lifelong friends. The other Leyrac children had remained in Chile.

In the chaos of the 1940 defeat, Adrien, now a wine merchant, met and married his wife Paulette. She was fervently Pétainist; her parents, both senior civil servants, became collaborators. Jean joined the Resistance but Adrien favoured Pétain until he was faced by a desperate dilemma. When the French police came looking for Jews in his block of flats, he saw a mother jump over the balcony with her two small children. He then felt he must join Jean in the Resistance. Paulette, however, away at the time, still refused to believe that arrested Jews were killed. Yet they both loved each other deeply and she was pregnant. Adrien, having made sure she would have enough money, left to join the Resistance, but was betrayed to the Gestapo and sent to Dachau, where he died. As Paulette blamed Jean for Adrien's death, she told Christian next to nothing about his father.

Christian had tried to understand both why his mother could ignore such horrors and how his father could abandon his pregnant wife. Jean points out that Adrien had to follow his conscience but that to stay at home would have endangered Paulette, so having failed to convince her, he left. Paulette, for her part, was mistaken in her views, but was honest and never tried to exploit Adrien's heroic status after the war.

The night he spends in a cell and the experience he has of a totalitarian regime help Christian to understand his parents better. He even suspects that his father may have left his Pétainist wife with her agreement and that at least her honesty made her refuse, at the Liberation, to join the turncoats, the 'vaillants pétaino-gaullistes' (*19*, p. 235). When he is set free next day, Christian treats Pinochet's officials with due contempt.

La Nuit de Calama has a double historical basis and brings the regional novels from which it springs into a wider dimension. It uses the relatively recent events of Pinochet's Chile in order to help readers, especially younger readers, to understand the Occupation of France, the complex problems it raised in everyday life and the dangers of totalitarianism. Adrien's dilemma recalls that of many people in difficult times for whom obeying their conscience is likely to bring death for themselves—which they may feel able to accept— but also danger for their loved ones, which is much harder to accept. That is why it was so hard for people to join the Resistance and why many of those who did so were doubly heroic, as were their families who were put at risk; when Edmond Michelet decided to join in setting up a Resistance group in Brive, he did so with the agreement of his wife and, no doubt, of his children. The situation is one which has a universal dimension.

Michelet's novel brings out well the complexities and dilemmas of life in wartime France and the different ways in which people reacted to intense pressure. He shows us not only how hard it was to opt for the Resistance and how easy it was not to, but also the fact that Pétainists, if sometimes naïve, were not all self-seeking. Those who earn his real scorn are the many who underwent instantaneous conversions to Gaullism at the Liberation. The plot is a clever and interesting one, with Christian as its lynchpin and a number of unexpected twists. The characters are perceptively and sensitively drawn: Jean's attempts to spare Christian's feelings about his parents during their conversation are a good example of this.

As in the other novels, the world is perceived through the values of the characters, but the central ones, those of Jean and Christian, with their denunciation of totalitarian regimes, wherever they may be, are clearly those of their creator. He believes it vitally important that the horrors of the last war, many of them repeated in Pinochet's Chile and elsewhere, should not be forgotten. The reason for this is not a desire to rejoice in militarism but the determination to do everything in his power to prevent such appalling deeds from ever happening again. Like Firmin going off to war in 1914, with equal seriousness but with a much clearer view of where justice and injustice lie, he believes that evil must be resisted; we must remember that he writes with the sound of his father being driven off to torture and imprisonment still in his ears. Recent events in the world, in Ruanda, Bosnia and elsewhere, together with the loss of his own son, underline his point and echo the solidity of his commitment.

Conclusion

Claude Michelet and the
roman régional

One of the most notable features of the French literary scene in
recent years has been the proliferation of novels set in particular
parts of the country and dealing with the life of people living there,
mostly in the first half of the twentieth century. The action usually,
but not invariably, takes place in a rural setting. This is very
understandable in the context of the enormous changes that have
taken place as the French population changed its character from
being still largely rural to being mainly urban; according to the
standard reference book, *Quid,* the total number of French people
engaged in agriculture dropped from over six million in 1955 to
under two million in 1990 and is expected to be little more than half
a million by the year 2000. In the same period, the population as a
whole had been increasing and reached 56.3 million in 1990.

The practical result of this has been that one set of problems—
those of an agriculture in decline—has been replaced by another,
only too familiar in Britain and elsewhere: those of urban
unemployment and the decaying inner city or, in the French case, the
banlieue. Many French men and women feel that something valuable
and important, for them at least, has disappeared in the process—and
it disappeared not all that long ago, in many cases. The nostalgia for
a lost heritage, the longing to rediscover their roots in a particular
region, is very real among people who, even though they were
brought up in a town, may still have memories of helping their
country cousins with the harvest on the old family farm in
Normandy or the Auvergne during the month's paid leave from a
factory in Paris or Clermont-Ferrand—not everyone could afford a
hotel when the Front populaire had introduced the *congés payés* in
1936. The beauty of the rural landscape, the wildlife, the variety of
the changing seasons, the sense of belonging to an extended family
and a village community have been lost for them in the dullness and
anonymity of the town. The drawbacks of the old life, of course,

tend to be glossed over or forgotten: the material poverty, the lack of comfort, the sheer hard grind of working life and being out in all weathers in the country. But in the end, the balance sheet seems to show a loss, all the more so if the move to the town, if relatively recent, was not made from choice.

The regional novel, then, brings back the memory of things past to those who once knew that way of life, if only during the holidays; it can also provide interesting points of comparison between the region the reader knows and that described in the novel she or he is reading. It can, moreover, help to satisfy the curiosity of younger readers as to how their grandparents lived, thus making them aware of their origins and giving them some sense of what made them what they are.

Seen in this perspective, to judge only from its sales figures, *La Grande Muraille* is clearly a successful regional novel, as are the books of the Saint-Libéral trilogy, which between them have already sold around six million copies. It is also clear, however, that amongst the plethora of works which the genre has produced recently, and continues to produce, not all come up to the same standard. This has induced certain critics to despise the genre as such. Yet the idea of a regional novel is a hard one to define with any precision. It would seem at least to imply that there is an intimate, even inseparable, connection between the work and its setting in a particular part of a country; in this case, of France. If, then, we look at two well-known masterpieces of the novel in this light, it is perhaps possible to imagine the action of *Madame Bovary* taking place in another province than Normandy, although its setting and the particular mentality of the local people who appear in it are hard to separate from its plot. It would, however, be extremely difficult to imagine Mauriac's characters (in particular, Thérèse Desqueyroux) as living elsewhere than amongst the pines of the Bordelais and in its rather particular society. Mauriac's novels would therefore definitely seem to be regional novels and *Madame Bovary* could, very arguably, also qualify as one.

When asked by me whether he was a regional novelist, Claude Michelet replied that whether a novel was called 'regional' or not was unimportant: what mattered was whether or not it was a good novel. The patronising attitude of some critics, who, as already mentioned, use the term 'regional' as a label with which to dismiss books which they did not like, had provoked himself and a number of friends—the aforementioned Jacques Peuchmaurd (*supra,* p. 52),

Michel Peyramaure, Christian Signol, Denis Tillinac—all well-known writers of novels set in the Corrèze or neighbouring regions and who meet at the book fair held annually in Brive, into feeling that they had to make some kind of protest (for more detail see *25,* pp. 172-5). They therefore decided, very much tongue in cheek, to adopt for themselves the somewhat pretentious title of 'L'École de Brive' used by a local journalist; if the Romantics, the Realists or the Surrealists could call themselves a school, why not they? Their main defect in the eyes of their detractors was perhaps the fact that their books had a wide appeal and sold well.

Many talented writers have lived and died in poverty, but the literary merit of an author's work is not necessarily in inverse proportion to its sales figures. The examples of Dickens, Thackeray, Balzac and many others are there to prove it. What is important is to examine the works and ask whether they deserve to succeed. I hope to have shown in the preceding chapters that the success of *La Grande Muraille* was well merited, as was the success of the novels that succeeded it. It must be abundantly clear by now that for all his popularity, Claude Michelet is no writer of 'pot-boilers', cheap romances or adventure stories. The form he uses for his novels may be a traditional one, but he uses it with great talent. His strengths lie in the age-old skills of delineating a character and telling a story. Many of the stories are set in the countryside, but he does not idealise either country people—the way in which Firmin is treated by his fellow-villagers illustrates that—or their way of life—as in his portrayal of the effects of the 1930s' slump in *Les Palombes ne passeront plus* or the economic plight of Michel and his wife in *Rocheflame.* Moreover he writes of such matters with the knowledge of an insider.

As has been said, he is particularly skilled at portraying ordinary people, across a wide sweep of society, and at conveying their feelings and sensitivities, even though they may not always be well educated and highly articulate. The ability to 'get inside' an 'ordinary' yet extraordinary character like Firmin, to bring him to life and to help the reader to understand and sympathise with him as he pursues his lonely task in face of the intolerance of his fellow villagers, is a rare one and easy to underestimate.

Claude Michelet is, then, much more than a 'mere' regional novelist and, as the variety of his plots and characters demonstrates, he is certainly not one who writes to a formula in order to attain the highest possible sales figures. Unlike many modern writers—popular and other—he does not attempt to exploit sex and violence; both are there, as they are in life, but the sex is nearly always loving and the violence is usually centred on war; it is, moreover, certainly not glorified. What does stand out in the novels, including the Chilean trilogy, is a deep interest in people, a passionate love of the land and a strong sense of history. All of these are ideas with which the reader, and especially the French reader, can identify. Claude Michelet's novels clearly appeal to something deep in the French psyche. His friend Pierre Panen speaks of him as being, politically, a Gaullist 'par filiation et par conviction', but 'un vrai gaulliste qui se méfie naturellement des appareils de parti' (25, p. 66). Indeed we have seen that his books express, in their own way, a kind of literary Gaullism, in the very best sense of that word. It is the idealistic Gaullism of the wartime years, urging French people—and others— of all opinions to unite against what is evil and unjust, to respect all of their fellow human beings, to reject the political and religious intolerance of the past and to strive for something better in the future.

Yet the idealism is not starry-eyed, for in the novels people are seen as they are, with all their good qualities and faults. The author clearly rejoices in what is good and honest in them and rejects, in particular, what is narrow-minded and hypocritical, yet he still accepts them all, for they are human as he is. His attitude is well illustrated by a passage in *Les Palombes ne passeront plus* which describes the arrival in Saint-Libéral, after the Liberation, of three young men who have come to arrest two alleged collaborators, one of them the *curé*. The villagers fiercely refuse to hand over their *curé*, however pro-Vichy he may have been, and they later testify on behalf of the other man, since he never betrayed anyone: for all their faults, both are still part of village society. (The rejection of Firmin by his fellow villagers in *La Grande Muraille*, like the delivery to the competent authorities of Maxime Loin in Marcel Aymé's *Uranus*, becomes all the more shameful in comparison). The ultimate values implicit in the works of Claude Michelet are those of decency and humanity as against totalitarianism and selfishness and his view of human nature is a positive, though not a falsely optimistic one. His voice is that of a man who was a child under the Occupation, who saw his own father arrested by the Gestapo, and whose childhood home itself, in Brive, is now a museum devoted largely to the story of the concentration camps. It is a voice which inspires respect.

Bibliography

The place of publication, unless otherwise stated, is Paris. It must be said that the English translations (9, 10 and 16), including their titles, leave much to be desired. My interview with Claude Michelet, which took place in Marcillac on 25 August 1994, is referred to in the text by the symbol *Int.*

Works by Claude Michelet

1. *La Terre qui demeure,* Le Moniteur agricole, 1965 (currently out of print).

2. *La Grande Muraille,* Julliard, 1969. Re-edited by Robert Laffont, 1981, and in Presses Pocket, 1983.

3. *Une fois sept,* Julliard, 1970; Laffont, 1983; Presses Pocket, 1986.

4. *Les Noces de sable,* a radio play for France Culture, 1972 (not seen by this author, but mentioned by P. Panen, *25,* p. 226).

5. *Mon père Edmond Michelet,* Presses de la Cité, 1971; Laffont 1981; Presses Pocket, 1990. Awarded Prix des Écrivains combattants, 1972.

6. *Rocheflame,* Julliard, 1973; Laffont, 1982; Presses Pocket, 1984.

7. *J'ai choisi la terre,* Laffont, 1975; Presses Pocket, 1981. Awarded Prix des Volcans, 1975.

8. *Cette terre est la vôtre,* Laffont, 1977; Presses Pocket, 1982. Republished by Laffont in 1988 as *Cette terre est toujours la vôtre* with new *Avant-propos* and articles published in *Agrisept* and *Le Nouvel Agriculteur* from 1979-1988.

9. *Des grives aux loups,* Laffont 1979; Presses Pocket 1982. Awarded Prix Eugène Le Roy, 1979, and Prix des Libraires, 1980. Translated into English as *Firelight and Woodsmoke,* Orion, 1993; Orion Paperback, 1994.

10. *Les Palombes ne passeront plus,* Laffont 1980; Presses Pocket 1982. Translated into English as *Applewood,* Orion Paperback, 1994.

11   *Les Promesses du ciel et de la terre,* Laffont, 1985; Presses Pocket, 1989.

12   *Pour un arpent de terre,* Laffont, 1986; Presses Pocket, 1992.

13.   *Le Grand Sillon,* Laffont, 1988; Presses Pocket, 1991.

14.   *Le Secret des Incas,* Bayard-Presse, 1989.

15.   *Vive l'heure d'hiver,* Renaudot, 1989; Presses Pocket, 1989.

16.   *L'Appel des engoulevents,* Laffont, 1990; Presses Pocket, 1992. English translation *Scent of Herbs,* Orion Paperback, 1994.

17.   *Les Cent Plus Beaux Chants de la terre,* Le Cherche-midi, 1990. An anthology, with introduction, of poems about the land, ranging from medieval times (Guillaume de Lorris) to the present day.

18.   *Quatre saisons en Limousin, propos de table et recettes,* written with Bernadette Michelet and illustrated by Yves Michelet, Laffont, 1992.

19.   *La Nuit de Calama,* Laffont, 1994.

20.   *Cette terre qui m'entoure; propos d'un Corrézien,* Laffont/ Christian de Bartillat, 1995. A conversation between Claude Michelet and Maurice Chavardès in which Michelet talks about the joys and problems of present-day rural life.

In addition, Claude Michelet contributed on a regular basis to *Le Moniteur agricole,* then to *Agrisept* and its successor *Le Nouvel Agriculteur.* He has also contributed short stories to *La Croix, L'Express, Télé 7 Jours,* etc. These are mentioned, with extracts given, by Pierre Panen (*25,* chapter 11).

Works by or about Edmond Michelet

21.   Charbonnel, Jean, *Edmond Michelet,* Collection 'Politiques et Chrétiens', Beauchesne, 1987.

22.   Michelet, Edmond, *Rue de la liberté,* Seuil, 1955.

23.   Panen, Pierre, *Edmond Michelet,* Desclée de Brouwer, 1991.

Works about Claude Michelet

24.   Dryhurst, James, 'Derrière *La Grande Muraille'*, *Francophonie*, 8 (December 1993), 30-40.

25.   Panen, Pierre, *Claude Michelet sur la terre des hommes*, Laffont, 1993; revised edition Presses Pocket, 1995.

26.   Parry, Margaret, *'Rocheflame*, an example of "green" literature', *Francophonie*, 3 (June 1991), 11-15.

Other Works

27.   Carles, Émilie, *Une soupe aux herbes sauvages*, Laffont, 1981; Livre de Poche, 1990.

28.   Péguy, Charles, *Œuvres en prose 1909-1914*, NRF Gallimard, 'Bibliothèque de la Pléiade', 1957.

Locations

The region in which Claude Michelet's novels are set is covered by the 1:25,000 *Série bleue* of the IGN (Institut Géographique National). The wall near Chartrier-Ferrière is to be found on map no. 2135 ouest (Brive-la-Gaillarde) at reference East 377.5, North 4992.1. Most of the locations mentioned in the Saint-Libéral trilogy are to be found on map no. 2034 est (Juillac).

The Michelets' old home in Brive (4, rue Champanatier, not far from the station) now houses the Centre National de la Résistance et de la Déportation Edmond Michelet. In addition to its most interesting and informative collection of exhibits, some horrifying (mostly those concerning the concentration camps) there is a valuable Centre de Documentation et de Recherche.